The Poet, the Lion,
Talking Pictures, El
Farolito, a Wedding
in St. Roch, the Big
Box Store, the Warp
in the Mirror, Spring,
Midnights, Fire & All

Also by C.D. Wright

The Poet, the Lion, Talking Pictures, El Farolito, a Wedding in St. Roch, the Big Box Store, the Warp in the Mirror, Spring, Midnights, Fire & All

C.D. Wright

COPPER CANYON PRESS
PORT TOWNSEND, WASHINGTON

Cover art: *Black Bush in Desert, #1,* by Denny Moers

Copper Canyon Press is in residence at Fort Worden State Park in Port Townsend, Washington, under the auspices of Centrum. Centrum is a gathering place for artists and creative thinkers from around the world, students of all ages and backgrounds, and audiences seeking extraordinary cultural enrichment.

LIBRARY OF CONGRESS CATALOGING-IN-PUBLICATION DATA

Wright, C.D., 1949–
  The Poet, the Lion, Talking Pictures, El Farolito, a Wedding in St. Roch, the Big Box Store, the Warp in the Mirror, Spring, Midnights, Fire & All / C.D. Wright.
    pages cm
  ISBN 978-1-55659-485-4 (paperback)
  1. Poetry. 2. Poetry—Authorship. 1. Title.
  PS3573.R497P64 2015
  814'.54—dc23
                          2015026869

98765432 FIRST PRINTING

COPPER CANYON PRESS

Post Office Box 271

Port Townsend, Washington 98368

www.coppercanyonpress.org

Acknowledgments

The writer would like to thank the editors associated with the following presses and journals from which certain passages and/or entire essays were chosen, as well as collaborators and writers and instigators who colluded with the texts:

Kazim Ali, who moderated the panel "Jean Valentine, Poet" at AWP, Denver, 2010.

Michael Barron at New Directions, for his editing of the foreword of the 2011 facsimile edition of William Carlos Williams's *Spring and All*.

Cal Bedient, publishing editor of *Lana Turner: A Journal of Poetry and Opinion*, no. 2 (2009).

Rachel Berchten at University of California Press.

Norman Boucher and Charlotte Harvey at *Brown Alumni Magazine*.

Lucie Brock-Broido at Columbia University, for a seminar platform (November 12, 2009).

Paul Ebenkamp and Robert Hass and Jack Shoemaker, Counterpoint Press.

Foundation for Contemporary Arts, 1999.

Brad N. Haas for his interviews with John Taggart in *FlashPoint* (September 13, 2001 & January 8, 2002).

H.L. Hix for his blog, *In Quire: A crossing point for ideas, words, images, and energies* (January 23 & 25, 2015).

Henry Israeli at Saturnalia Books.

Joshua Kotin and Robert P. Baird at *Chicago Review*, for a two-part publication of "During the Composition of 'Rising, Falling, Hovering,'" 53, no. 4 & 54, nos. 1/2 (Summer 2008).

Marshall Walker Lee, Drew Scott Swenhaugen, and the rest of the cast at *Poor Claudia*, no. 3 (2010).

Michael Ondaatje, for his poem "Driving with Dominic / in the Southern Province / We See Hints of the Circus," from *Handwriting* (Alfred A. Knopf, 1999).

Claudia Rankine and Lisa Sewell, for *Eleven More American Women Poets in the 21st Century* (Wesleyan University Press, 2012).

Michael Redhill and Michael Ondaatje, *BRICK*, no. 91 (Summer 2013); Michael Redhill, *BRICK*, no. 92 (Winter 2014).

Cláudia Roquette-Pinto, for translating "Of Those Who Can Afford to Be Gentle" and placing it in *Revista Confraria: Arte e literatura* (Rio de Janeiro, Brazil), no. 17 (November & December 2007).

Marc Smirnoff at *Oxford American*, no. 62 (Autumn 2008).

The Squaw Valley Community of Writers, time and again.

Peter Streckfus-Green, who moderated the panel "Prose and Verse Consubstantial: The New Mixed Form" at AWP, Boston, 2013.

Brian Teare at Albion Books, for publishing *Jean Valentine, Abridged* (2011).

Michael Wiegers at Copper Canyon Press, time and time again, and for persuading me to write the preface, "Stripe for Stripe," for the text edition of *One Big Self* (2007) and for inviting me to write the foreword to John Taggart's selected poems, *Is Music* (2010).

Joshua Marie Wilkinson at *Evening Will Come: A Monthly Journal of Poetics*, no. 1 (2011).

Andrew Zawacki, for editing *Poetry Northwest: The Photography Issue*, 8, no. 1 (Spring & Summer 2013).

I would also like to thank Deborah Luster, for including me in her project on Louisiana prisons.

I would finally like to thank President Christina H. Paxson and the members of her committee, for inviting me to deliver the inaugural Presidential Faculty Award Lecture at Brown University (October 29, 2013), passages from which are incorporated in this book.

for Nadia Moss and Susie Schlesinger

in memory of Evan S. Connell

Suppose I'd been an alligator, I might enjoy the situation more

EVAN S. CONNELL

Contents

The Poet, the Lion,
Talking Pictures, El
Farolito, a Wedding
in St. Roch, the Big
Box Store, the Warp
in the Mirror, Spring,
Midnights, Fire & All

In a Word,
a World

I love them all.

I love that a handful, a mouthful, gets you by, a satchelful can land you a job, a well-chosen clutch of them could get you laid, and that a solitary word can initiate a stampede, and therefore can be formally outlawed — even by a liberal court bent on defending a constitution guaranteeing unimpeded utterance. I love that the Argentine gaucho has over two hundred words for the coloration of horses and the Sami language of Scandinavia has over a thousand words for reindeer based on age, sex, appearance — e.g., a *busat* has big balls or only one big ball. More than the pristine, I love the filthy ones for their descriptive talent as well as transgressive nature. I love the dirty ones more than the minced, in that I respect extravagant expression more than reserved. I admire reserve, especially when taken to an ascetic *n*th. I love the particular lexicons of particular occupations. The substrate of those activities. The nomenclatures within nomenclatures. I am of the unaccredited school that believes animals did not exist until Adam assigned them names. My relationship to the word is anything but scientific; it is a matter of faith on my part, that the word endows material substance, by setting the thing named apart from all else. *Horse,* then, unhorses what is not horse.

My American Scrawl

Increasingly indecisive, about matters both big and little, I have found that poetry is the one arena where I am not inclined to crank up the fog machine, to palter or dissemble or quaver or hastily reverse myself. This is the one scene where I advance determined, if not precisely ready, to do battle with what an overly cited Jungian described as the anesthetized heart, the heart that does not react.

Hold Still, Lion

What you do is how you get along.
What you did is all it ever means.

"Place to Be"

By the time I knew Robert Creeley well enough to call him my friend, the notorious one-eyed scrapper bard had long become poetry's emblem of bonhomie. A mundane sandwich with Bob would prompt a swift e-mail, "Thanks again for the good company and soul-securing lunch." Speaking to him on the phone on the 25th of March, 2005, and getting a straightforward sense of his condition, I wrote simply that I loved him. The next morning came, "Thanks for that reassuring information! One quick question, do you guys know a simple lawyer there in the 'Providence area'? We need to make a new will, since we've changed residence from NY to RI. Always something to do! Love to you all." Bob famously loved the Internet. Small wonder. Finally some *thing* actually existed that could facilitate his wonderful rapid-fire mind and keep him in touch with his ever-widening affections.

A Plague of Poets

A question posed to Flannery O'Connor, as to whether writing programs stifled writers, drew the famous, tart rejoinder that in her opinion they didn't stifle nearly enough.

Even if, as it is often said, there are too many of us — poets, that is — that the field is too crowded (as opposed to too many hedge-fund managers or too many pharmaceutical lobbyists or too many fundamentalists), time, rejection, discouragement, and the inevitable practicalities and detours (some of them fortuitous), as well as wasted energy, the slow seepage or sudden shift of interest, premature death, burdensome debt or better offers, usually cure the problem of overpopulation. In other words, there are plenty of natural predators.

The Book That Jane Wrote
Midnights

Poetry is nothing if not equipped for crisis. Sharp and penetrating, it cuts through every fear by which we are secretly governed, brings each to the light of the page and names it. *Total exposure*. Anything less is not an option, not if "[you] want to live in the world in [your] right mind." The poet does. Even so, the lovers will part, the mother begin to die. Losses, Gentle Reader, will mount.

+ + +

Jasmine, lavender, blended vintages, a spray of fine perfume, Camembert cheese, big pink California roses overflow the set. Wherever Jane Miller goes, the senses will gather.

+ + +

The goal is to make not sense but art of this story. The goal is not to make a story but to experience the whole mess. There are mental sufferings and physical sufferings to go through — to apprehend if one can. There are the spent casings of history to sift through, pick up, and examine. Calm-like, hysterical, forensic. This life is not just a worn passage.

Nuptials & Violence

for Deborah Luster & Kevin Sullivan

Each place continues to yield its own quiddities, its own miraculous movements, and its own tragedies. "Everywhere there is has everything there is to look at," wrote poet Bernadette Mayer. So Deborah Luster visits places with which she has some identification, some familiarity, places that speak to her in the most immediate terms. Individuals emerge from those places in their particular lineaments. Every picture strives to shorten the distance between "us" and "them."

+ + +

The true function of poetry [art], said Allen Grossman, is to keep the image of persons as precious in the world. Everywhere there is has everything there is to look at. Asked whether Deborah considered her new body of work, *Tooth for an Eye: A Chorography of Violence in Orleans Parish,* more futile or more beautiful, she responded: Equal parts futile and beautiful.

Stripe for Stripe

Driving through this part of Louisiana you can pass four prisons in less than an hour. "The spirit of every age," writes Eric Schlosser, "is manifest in its public works." So this is who we are, the jailers, the jailed. This is the spirit of our age.

"You won't be back will you," asked the inmate who told me he wanted to be a success.

+ + +

Try to remember it the way it was. Try to remember what I wore when I visited the prisons. Trying to remember how tall was my boy then. What books I was teaching. Trying to remember how I hoped to add one true and lonely word to the host of texts that bear upon incarceration.

Something about the extra-realism of that peculiar institution caused me to balk, also the resistance of poetry to the conventions of evidentiary writing, notwithstanding top-notch examples to the contrary: Mandelstam, Akhmatova, Wilde, Valéry, Celan, Desnos, et al. After all, I am not *them*. She asked me to come down, my friend the photographer, and I went, and then I wanted to see whether my art could handle that hoe.

Trying to remember how my skin felt when I opened an envelope of proofs of Deborah Luster's intimate aluminum portraits of the inmates at Transylvania (the site of East Carroll Parish Prison Farm, a minimum-security male prison, now closed); then Angola (the site of Louisiana State Penitentiary, maximum security, ever-growing); then St. Gabriel (the site of the Louisiana Correctional Institution for Women, the LCIW). I was electrified by the first face—a young, handsome man blowing smoke out of his nose. Behind every anonymous number, a very specific face.

On the phone my friend had described to me the rich Delta grounds of Angola, 18,000 acres. Angola, where the topsoil is measured not in inches but feet. The former sugarcane plantation lies at the confluence of rivers and borderland of the vermin-and-vine-choked Tunica Hills. Grey pelicans nest on the two prison lakes; alongside the airstrip are the grading sheds, the endless fields of okra and corn. Then there's the prison museum, the prison radio station, the prison monthly magazine; the tracking horses and tracking dogs trained by inmates… and the tree-lined neighborhood of free-world residents, their children bused outside the fence to school. Then the immaculate cinderblock buildings that house the inmates, the administration building, and the death house; the greenhouse and extensive flower beds—take away the fencing and it resembles nothing so much as a college campus. The men in maximum number more than the men who lived in my hometown. Then there's the geriatric unit, the award-winning hospice program; the caisson the inmates built to bear the dead in the hand-built coffins to one of the two graveyards inside the prison. In the old burial ground most graves are not identified by name. The caisson is pulled by draft horses, French Quarter style. When the champion of the prison rodeo had a heart attack in the fields, a riderless horse led the final procession. The celebrated inmate's uniform was "retired" to the prison museum.

Everything about Louisiana seems to constitute itself differently from everywhere else in the Union: the food, the idiom, the stuff in the trees, the critters in the water, and the laws, Napoleonic, not mother-country common law. The prisons inevitably mirror differences found in the free world. Where they came up with their mirrors is another mystery. (In maximum, they are made of metal.) The definition of the face is a memory.

Vivid to me is Debbie saying that at the trial of her mother's murderer, she looked around and saw the people sitting on separate sides of the courtroom, the way they do at a wedding, the bride's people, the groom's people, and she tried to take in the damage radiating through the distinct lines—the perpetrator's side, the victim's side.

Vivid to me is leaving Angola after the first visit and Debbie asking what I thought, and I said (too fast) I thought those were the nicest people I had ever met, and the ironic laughter it provoked in us both, the car yawing. The obvious truth, people are people. Equally, the damage is never limited to perpetrator and victim. Also, that the crimes are not the sum of the criminal any more than anyone is entirely separable from their acts.

I remember an afternoon at the iron pile at Transylvania watching the men quietly plait each other's hair between sets at the weight bench. When I asked about a man whose face was severely scarred, a very specific face, with large, direct aquamarine eyes, a guard told me that the man's brother had thrown a tire over his head and set it on fire. This I did not know how to absorb. It was a steaming day; the men were lifting weights and plaiting their hair.

I remember Easter weekend at the women's prison. The day before, a long line formed outside the prison-run beauty shop. Inside, the women having their hair fixed were talking back to a soap opera on the small snowy screen. By visiting day the inner courtyard had been transformed into a theme park for the children. A trampoline had been rented, a cotton-candy machine; someone dressed in a bunny suit was organizing an egg hunt. The girls wore starched, flouncy dresses, and the boys white jackets and black, clip-on bow ties. The women were dressed up, too, even the ones shackled at ankle and waist. Deborah photographed all day, nonstop. Identifiable pictures of children would have to be excluded from publication, but people wanted a keepsake. We left before visiting hours ended. It wasn't our place to be there. It wasn't really in us to be there.

Remember sitting in the frigid Holiday Inn bar near St. Gabriel, at the end of one visit to the women's prison, staring at the aquarium, not talking.

Talking to a man who says he has done a lot of time. Lot of time. He should write a book, he says. He wants to be a success. "Hollywood, huh, here I come."

Talking to a woman who says the one time her dad visited her from the Midwest, she asked him to look at her eyes. There was a look she didn't want to get, a faraway look. Her father pretended to examine her eyes, then told her they looked like the same old peepers to him. She passed her time reading. Same way she passed her childhood. She thought she was going to be an astronomer when she grew up. Not a felon.

Both parents are dead now. Of her three sons, one disappeared, one died of suicide, and the third severed contact.

One of the inmates at St. Gabriel informed me she wouldn't be around for visiting hours tomorrow because she was on the drill team. Also, her ex-husband would not be bringing her baby boy to see her. Not tomorrow, not ever.

The grease burns, I am told by another inmate, are courtesy of her sister.

Don't Walk On The Grass, says the sign posted in the inner yard.

The coffin builder in the prison was so devoted to his Catahoula he overfed her to the point that she could walk only side to side. She wore a red halter he fashioned for her. Sissy was the dog's name. His name was Redwine. He wore a colostomy bag. Both Sissy and Mr. Redwine have since passed. Inside.

The inmate who fishes one of the stocked lakes for the warden admitted that his son was in prison, too, in another state. He saw him once when he was a baby. And then, once, between sentences.

A guard pointed out a woman whose father, mother, uncle, brother, and sister were all locked up, two were at Hunt, two here, and one at Big Gola. Her sister was her fall partner. It made you wonder who was left to look after the dog.

That day Debbie was photographing mothers and daughters, and twins.

Another guard told me he had made the mistake he had most dreaded making, delivering the execution letter, setting the date and the time, to the wrong man on death row.

In some prisons, you can't have a last cigarette, but Valium is permitted.

I heard about a petition in a town out West to take back the night sky. The locals thought they were getting a second minimum-security prison, an economic pick-me-up. Instead, a supermax sprang up, that perverse marriage of mind and technology. Lights from the new institution burn so intensely the stars have gone dark on them.

Then there's the bus that leaves from Monroe taking visitors to one of four neighboring pens, Al Derry's Prison Transport and Popcorn Balls. Evidently, the popcorn balls make it the competitive ride. Only in Louisiana.

After a time. A lot of time. They stop coming. The free-worlders. They are too poor or too busy working or are already looking after others on the outside or their car is broken or they are too worn down or they move too far off or they get old, sick, and die. So the inmates wait for their turn.

They aren't going anywhere. They have all the time there is.

"The only continuity of our lives," wrote Malcolm Braly, American writer, American lifer, "was that we had none."

"Waiting," goes the motto at St. Gabriel, "it's the LCIW way."

I wrote a woman and asked whether she ever had any pets. She wrote back: Bandit, Baby, Snobby, Elsie, Bear (those were the dogs). Tiger and Fuzzball (the cats), Jill, Ben, and Junior (the coons). And a lot of unnamed fish, hamsters, rabbits, chickens, ducks, geese, guinea pigs, "and a deer, not really a pet but I finally coaxed to the point she would eat out of my hand."

Not to idealize, not to judge, not to exonerate, not to aestheticize immeasurable levels of pain. Not to demonize, not anathematize. What I wanted was to unequivocally lay out the real feel of hard time. I wanted it given to understand that when you pass four prisons in less than an hour, the countryside's apparent emptiness is more legible. It is an open, running comment when the only spike in employment statistics is being created by the supply of people crossing the line.

I wanted the banter, the idiom, the soft-spoken cadence of Louisiana speech to cut through the mass-media myopia. I wanted the heat, the humidity, the fecundity of Louisiana to travel right up the body. What I wanted was to convey the sense of normalcy for which humans strive under conditions that are anything but what we in the free world call normal, no matter what we may have done for which we were never charged.

The world of the prison system springs up adjacent to the free world. As the towns decline, the prisons grow. As industries disappear, prisons proliferate, state-funded prison-building surges are complemented by private-investment promising "to be an integral component of your corrections strategy," according to an industry founder. The interrelation of poverty, illiteracy, substance and physical abuse, mental illness, race, and gender to the prison population is blaring to the naked eye and borne out by the statistics. Of the developed nations, only Russia aspires to our rate of incarceration. And the Big Bear is a distant second. Ladies and Gentlemen of the Jury, the warp in the mirror is of our making.

The popular perception is that art is apart. I insist it is a part of. Something not in dispute is that people in prison are apart from. If you can accept — whatever level of discipline and punishment you adhere to momentarily set aside — that the ultimate goal should be to reunite the separated with the larger human enterprise, it might behoove us to see prisoners, among others, as they elect to be seen, in their larger selves. If we go there, if not with our bodies then at least our minds, we are more likely to register the implications.

+ + +

I am going to prison.

I am going to visit three prisons in Louisiana.

I am going on the heels of my longtime friend Deborah Luster, a photographer.

It is a summons.

All roads are turning into prison roads.

I already feel guilty.

I haven't done anything.

But I allow the mental pull in both directions.

I am going to prison in order to write about it. Like a nineteenth-century traveler.

Kafka put it this way, "Guilt is never to be doubted."

Also: behind every anonymous number, a very specific face.

Also: there are more than two million individuals, in this country, whose sentences
    have rendered them more or less invisible. Many of them permanently.

First to Transylvania. Then Angola. Then St. Gabriel. These are their place-names.

Over the next year and a half Deborah Luster will photograph upwards of 1,500
    inmates.

I will make three trips.

It is an almost imperceptible gesture, a flick of the conscience, to go, to see, but I
    will be wakeful.

It is a summons.

Poems are my building projects. I inhabit them for the time it takes to have every corner lit, and then I clear out, taking what I think I need to start over. Invariably I have forgotten something I could really use; so I have to make do or figure out an unfamiliar, irregular means to make the next structure. Sometimes I work in discrete units; other times I work on an extended complex. Less and less am I persuaded by the medium's essence, and more and more I am pulled by its mutability. In recent years I have worked on various projects with photographer Deborah Luster. We are both restless in our processes, and stable in our sensibilities. We are both interested in exploring the possible ways by which you can make meaningful contact with a consciousness other than your own without surrendering the possibilities to an obvious common ground. Ideally the result will be spacious, fierce, strange, homey, humorous, tragic, etc., etc., an Earth station where almost anything can take place. More are welcome than can fit inside. I am not averse to torching a place that is not habitable (so long as no one is inside). I will uncover a use for the ashes.

Jean Valentine, Abridged

Watching Jem Cohen's film of Anne Truitt and seeing the retrospective of her work at the Hirshhorn, watching Mary Lance's film of Agnes Martin and reading Lisa Donovan's manuscript inspired by her paintings, have no doubt influenced this brief consideration of Jean Valentine. It seems fitting to respond to the poet with their company in the mute background. These three are artists who have spent their longish lives finding their proportions, setting their corners, mapping, if you will, the clear lines of an imagination.

+ + +

If Agnes Martin was trying to paint "the emotions we feel when we see grey geese descending," and Anne Truitt was aiming to make her pieces sing from the inside by her very particular use and usage of "laying down color" and "lifting color"— what has Jean Valentine been proposing to achieve with her formally and verbally spare creations? I submit that, like them, she aims for transparency, like them she starts "out of a feeling," but she is not interested in working it through by means of her story. In words, narrative is ultimately inescapable, but scattered elements of it will get the job done. Rather, she is organizing her emotions, in color terms, by their value—that is, by the darkness staved, the light given off.

Purgatorio

Raúl Zurita, it has been said, never writes about the coup; Raúl Zurita, it has been said, writes only about the coup. *Purgatorio* is arguably *the* seminal literary text of Chile's 9/11/1973, the date of the U.S.-backed military coup led by Augusto Pinochet which overthrew the democratically elected government of Salvador Allende. With his first published collection, the young Chilean poet began his Dantean trilogy, his long, arduous pilgrimage toward earthly redemption. "Even if the evidence at hand might indicate that such a pursuit is folly," Zurita later wrote, "we should keep on proposing Paradise."

+ + +

His *obra* began in conflict. The poet tormented his own image. He countered his self-loathing with an aspiration for divine love. He set his words at odds with one another — angels versus bitches, humble supplication versus invective, unbrokenness versus desperation — and out of a lose-lose situation he wrote a profanely transcendent book. In Spanish, this fiery, elliptical work has stayed in print since its debut six years into the Pinochet dictatorship.

In a Word, a World

I know the adjective can be a nuisance, and the adverb clumsy. I am a touch sick of the poetic inflation around prepositions. I would prefer that conjunctions were less visibly functional. Articles can clutter. The verb works the hardest. It should be the best paid. And I know fifteenth letter *O* is the best of all: O my black frying pan. O my fallen arches. O my degenerating fibroids. O what's the point. O little man at the foot of my bed, please don't steal my pillow.

Listening to John's
Is Music

My first slow-dance with John Taggart's poetry was *Conjunctions 10:* "Marvin Gaye Suite."

I didn't know who John Taggart was, but I was cutting my R&B teeth in Memphis, Tennessee, when Marvin Gaye was The Man.

What's going on. What's going on, people.

John Taggart was born not in Guthrie Center but Perry, Iowa.

Raised in small towns in Indiana. Son of a preacher man. Straight-up Protestant. Nothing serpent-kissy or glossolalicky.

When my family was moving to Iowa City for a year, Taggart called up those unforgiving Midwestern winters:

"We had to tie a rope from the house to the barn, so we could make our way to the barn and back."

"We had to beat the cows with brooms to keep them from freezing to death."

(It could have been horses. Equally horrifying.)

He started the influential *Maps* when he was an undergraduate.

Went to Earlham College with the good Quakers. His senior thesis was on Wallace Stevens.

He wasn't sure what Mr. Stevens was talking about, but it sounded like some cool beans. It wasn't long before young Taggert hit upon Mr. Bronk.

What's going on here.

A fellowship to the Aspen Writers' Workshop. A kid meeting writers: Toby Olson, Paul Blackburn, Bobby Byrd. His initiation had begun.

Early on, unlike some not-so-early-to-rise, he knew he wanted to be a writer.

He had in mind to write fiction. French fiction.

Even new French fiction required getting people in and out of cars and clothes, opening doors, rounding corners — some sign of a narrator. So lifelike.

"The furniture-moving aspects" of writing did not really appeal to him.

He wanted to get down on his knees with the language and dig with both hands.

An M.A. from the University of Chicago. A Ph.D. from Syracuse. He wrote his dissertation on Zukofsky.

Admits to growing a touch tired of Zukofsky (dissertations are famous for letting the air out). Z's coldness esp. (that, too, a kind of contraction). And growing more interested in Oppen. Just as exacting, but warmer.

The Taggart house in the Cumberland Valley. We visited once. It is the temperature of the place preserved in memory, the serrated air. The rushing cold millrace across the road from their house. The black birches.

The scoured dark inside the covered bridge. The covered bridge of Cumberland County. Its marvelous structure:

"the truss principle + arch… the structure is / what matters the flower the music of it." (See "Pastorelle 14.")

His collection of meticulously kept tools. "The careful workman." (See "Eroded Rock, 1942.")

He gave our son, who was around seven then, a fine, old bone-handled knife.

I gave my son, who is grown now, my father's fine, old bone-handled knife.

His love of the grid. Until it all but disappears in its penciled traces. (He cites Agnes Martin.)

A fondness for musical forms, of the searching variety: *ricercar*. (See eponymously titled poem.)

Partial to simple nouns. One syllable, "child the most basic word most haunting word" (see "In True Night"); two syllables, "crystal is a basic word crystal not paradise" (ibid.). Not more than two, unless there is a *necessary* polysyllable no one could have seen coming: *pantherine* (see "The Lily Alone").

How did we get along without it. What's going on here, Marvin.

Easy to assemble his *company keepers* (so the lifer I met at Angola called his roses).

Taggart's roses: writers, musicians, painters, and other artists. William Bronk, George Oppen, Susan Howe, Michael Palmer, Louis Zukofsky, Robert Creeley; Elvin Jones, John Coltrane, Thelonious Monk, Sonny Rollins; Marvin Gaye, Al Greene, Betty Carter, Sister Rosetta Tharpe, Clara Ward; Mark Rothko, Edward Weston, R.B. Kitaj (a shortened list). Also actual rugosas, of the should-not/must-pick varieties.

Those egghead Objectivists. Those Black Mountain cats. Those big-bosomed blues singers.

Just three words from Thomas Bernhard could set him off. A line from Thomas Traherne. Well, yeah.

Then a name that doesn't quite fit the grid, Robert Quine, ur-punk guitarist who played strong and strange for a lot of people who sucked up the glory: Richard Hell, Lou Reed, and so on.

A little poking around turns up Quine the same age as Taggart, attending Earlham, same as Taggart. I doubt that young Taggart missed much, certainly not an offensive noise escaping a dorm window.

Susceptible to the homage, the elegy, the ekphrastic. None of the terms satisfy the overall condition of this writing, esp. *ekphrastic,* which is fitting and lacking in an irritating way.

An inveterate letter writer. He continues to write his letters by hand, the script running perpendicular to the lines on the paper. It is a kind of scoring. And a kind of drawing.

Equally compositions and drawings.

I would say squarely in the tradition of writers whose letters are a highly reflective art in and of themselves.

The words are always moving, choosing phrases, singing. "To sing is to be untied." (See "Rhythm and Blues Singer.")

I am sure one knife is lost by now. More than likely, both.

The Objectivists could make things stop, stand out, and give no quarter. You would have to beat them with brooms to get them to lift a limb.

Taggart likes motion:

> Time for some passion in this language it's time to move
> it's time to move to make a move ma — mah — moo-euve-veh
> …let's waltz
>
> (See "The Rothko Chapel Poem.")

His signature repetition (see "Slow Song for Mark Rothko," "Giant Steps," "Peace on Earth," "Marvin Gaye Suite," and so on). "Augustine on repetition: a mode of assuring the seeker that he is on his way, and is not merely wandering blindly through the chaos from which all form arises" (see "Were You").

Affinity for the infinitive: to breathe, to sing, to light, to give, to hold out, to stretch, to straighten, to rise, to hold out to, to take, to take into the light, to be in light, to take as the host takes, to join, to end the silence and solitude, to take into intimacy… (see "Slow Song for Mark Rothko").

The closely monitored palette. "Forget violet." (See "Were You.") He chooses dark true colors. Ever-deepening. He likes to build them up on his blade.

Breath. That's a big topic, Marvin.

"Were you ready to listen and to understand in the gaps." (See "Were You.")

Listening to the scratch of his pen, the ping of his carriage, the bass of the speakers being balanced, the roar of his chainsaw in the snag tree, and rock being laid upon rock. "The careful workman."

I was swept right up in the poem's sampling of Marvin Gaye's hits and spiraling decline, his terrible end by his father's hand. The voice carrying on and on, multitracking, lustrous and fine, feminine but with pheromones coming right out of the armpit, making the listener, making every wandering onlooker ("moving with the wrong rhythm on the wrong beat") want to cry. I was hooked.

A Reader for Every Writer

The numbers are dispiriting, certainly from the book industry's perspective, and it is their sad obligation to track the numbers. Though I've never read *The Gutenberg Elegies,* I have long been afflicted with those post-Gutenberg blues. Yet I am privileged to talk to people almost every day who read deeply and widely, and when I step outside of that special circle, I can get an instant case of the willies, but am propelled in another instant to interact, to attune to the copious dimensions of living. The call of the writer is the same as the call of the reader. Take me to other planes of myself. Agnes Martin said her paintings were for people to look at *before daily care strikes.* Suppose reading and writing do their best work *after daily care has struck* (and struck hard).

Movies, paintings, and books stream through the poet's memory vault. They are called in "not [to] confuse reality but illumine it." Perhaps to contribute a few cues—how to live, how to endure. Poetry's privileged perch is not stable. "Poetry is speech by someone who is in trouble," is one poet's definition. There are more elegant definitions, but this one points to its primal aspect. Experience need not be assimilated. Art need not be separated. The poet would bid Virginia Woolf rise out of the Ouse emptying the stones from her pockets. She would that artists endure.

Hold Still, Lion

The years in which I spent the most time with Robert Creeley were the last ones. In his company I felt poetry's sturdiness and purpose. The solid barns and stone walls of New England come to mind. And that old, comforting word, *hearth*. "He was a great provider" is the phrase once used of a man who brought home the bacon. The phrase applies to Bob in the amplitude of the word: he provided for his family, he provided for his company, and he was concerned that his provisions be adequate. Meaning he cared *for* what he cared *about:* his family, the human family, and poetry, the family of poetry. It was a big charge. And he endeavored to make ready for a time when he could not be the active agent of so much responsibility. As Hank Lazer wrote from Alabama, "Without Bob here to be the figure of Onward, we must take what we have learned from him and be, in our writing and friendship and conversation and correspondence, that no longer singular figure of Onward." No one asked him to assume such a role, but no one else took it on, and he stepped up. He stepped up. When a young man, he acquired a reputation for his intellect, his talking, his humor, his temper, and for all the other uncurbed excesses of a nervous, cerebral, alienated American male.

In the last large third of his life, he was otherwise occupied. He always wanted to do things right. Now, he wanted to do the right thing. He wanted to get it all right:

> Hold still, lion!
> I am trying
> to paint you
> while there's time to.

Photography is by definition mute. It moves in on its object and kicks out all the racket. Poetry is not a particularly collaborative art—it is an acceptable occupation for the eye, to have a dialogue with its own mind. What happens when two people who work in distinct media form an alliance?

Her unfinished narratives against (as in *beside*) *her* unfinished landscapes. *Her* formal portraits alongside (as in *against*) *her* informal fragments. They are not looking for equivalents in each other's work, but for ways to enter the vacuums. Do they complete each other? In honesty, as in death, each goes it alone. One does not *require* the other, though in their shiniest skin they commingle.

At the level of the soles, the impulse toward joint artistic efforts often springs from a friendship that extends to a kindred sensibility, an ethos, a funny bone inscribed with identical numbers, an aesthetic that meshes—without too much ado. Collaboration offers an opportunity to break out of the isolation of one's own overly familiar braincase, an opportunity to have an experience that can't be got on one's own. Common projects do not forfeit the force of individual vision; they bring something else, a third direction, one that refuses to submit to *my way or the highway*. Whether new lineaments of truth are to be found in this kind of synergy, who knows.

Concerning Why Poetry Offers a Better Deal Than the World's Biggest Retailer

Today.

The poem stands alone.

But it is not made of itself alone. It is not brought into being by parthenogenesis. Not endowed with that level of self-sufficiency or self-concern. It gets it on with all the other arts. It communes with the non-arts. It strives for discipline. It never surrenders its wild streak. For some of the makers it is virtually on tap; for others it is like opening a vein. Whatever it takes, it takes. Whatever it gives, is also taken. Once made it has a degree of autonomy and with that comes the terrible face of isolation from having been made and having no sphere. From having only its own space to occupy.

Is this it then? The consumption of all by one? Does Walmart win?

Not so many are required to constitute a sphere, but enough to girdle, say, the great tree of Tule.

Poetry moves by indirection and in so doing avoids the crowd. This does not mean it would not draw others in. But one has to be responsive to its movement. One has to adjust to its unfamiliar configurations. One has to train one's best ear on its retrofitted lyre.

Poets do not create the environment in which their works would be received. Born in Somalia. Born in the Autonomous Region. Born in Arkansas, raised by the grace of God to be a razorback. Born to be a greeter at Walmart.

Indirection makes the circle hard to draw. It changes the route, and often the destination.

The inquiry poetry postulates remains intact. An inquiry extended along the lengths of the lines of knowing and beyond the tips of the known. Poetry figures the field of questions because it is never satisfied with the answers being so efficiently distributed as to capture the whole consumer base. Poetry it turns out, not capital, is what is fluid.

What if, one poet asks another poet, in a flash of foreboding, what if this is just *middle* capitalism?

Most manners and habits of thinking degenerate around the base. The forces — as I choose to call THEM — drive thinking away from its vast holdings, especially thinking variously. Rendering the base all solid- and smooth-seeming. Poetry tries to insinuate itself in the cracks. It tries to initiate cracks where all appeared heretofore imperturbable.

The language of poetry specializes in doubt. Without the doubters, everyone is cut off at the first question. Poetry does not presume to know, but is angling to get a glimpse of what is gradually coming into view; it aims to rightly identify what is looming; it intends to interrogate whatever is already in place. Poetry, whose definition remains evasive by necessity, advocates the lost road; and beyond speech — waiting, listening, and silence.

Some would blame poetry for being sidelined; some would blame forces beyond its control. Some would say poetry saved them from a life of futility, degradation, and despair, but this consequence cannot be measured in running feet. Some would say poetry alone had secured the relationship between their perceptions and their experience. I say, follow the money.

Not so long ago, it is fair to suggest, American poetry enjoyed an air of respectability. Like most important spheres, it persisted as an almost-exclusively white man's preserve. Even when it was composed by the madman or the drunkard, the poet himself might be written up, rewarded, even revered. A poet was a minor, secular god. Until the moment when he was caught driving backward on the main road, he was in command of his own field of ears. Then, blackout.

And there were, in those halcyon times, important arbiters to flush out the important voices, ensuring that a tiny number entered the tiny chamber, who could then be introduced to the great halls of the selectively schooled. And then did the art matter (to the selectively schooled).

Blame it on democracy; well, that grand philosophy has been put to the barbecue. Poets came out in swarms once the bell rang for them, but readers moved away in ever-greater numbers. Distraction trumps concentration. We knew this even before Mr. Walter Benjamin told us so. And nothing is more distracting than buying a ginormous pallet of stuff. Mr. Sam Walton did not even have to say it. Step onto the back of your shiny cart and take a roll down Action Alley. You need never run out of the things you never knew you wanted.

A common charge is that poetry is an internal affair—meaning poets partake of poetry; nonpoets would not be caught in its light. In view of our proliferation (a consequence or a casualty of its democratization, depending on your perspective), it doesn't mean there are not enough to complete the circle — that there are not enough to reinforce the circle. As Leonard Cohen put it, poetry is the opiate of the poets; but therein the circle threatens to close in on itself, and thus the boundaries begin to harden. And herein lies Walmart's great advantage: ever growing. And herein lies poetry's endurance: determination at the core.

In 2006, the Poetry Foundation published a survey and concluded there is an abundance of poetry "users." Only a modest 10 percent of those surveyed admitted to being "non-users." And more than half of the users know the title of a poem. (No comment.) Among non-users it is conceded that poetry may add something valuable to life, but just how they would know this is beyond the reach of this survey.

I say, read the children poetry.

If the competition is killing us, it is weirdly killing everything else, too — the water, the air, the recipe for Coca-Cola; it's even killing competition. Why spare "the best words in the best order"? Walmart rules.

As traditional forums for literary dissemination confront their own pressures, poetry can no longer be assigned filler space (apart from the publications created and maintained solely for the genre). In the process of disappearing from traditional media, poets have been as busy as every other enterprise in redirecting energy to the Internet — where the vitality of the practice is evident, but where the suffusion of word and image tends to minimize distinctions. Distinctions not just between good and bad but also between this and that, between now and never, between memory and forgetting, and so on. That hits do not necessarily translate as readers is obvious. However, hits do signal converging lines of curiosity. Hits also encompass actual readers. And hits combined with blogs and poemfilms enlarge the circle.

Entrepreneurs are not interested, period. When Steve Jobs said people don't read anymore, he could have been just taking a reflexive swipe at the competition (in this instance, Kindle), or he may have been merely musing aloud about his own habits (reading not being one of them), or worse, kissing off the beautiful dark schist of reflective thought. A couple of years prior to the Poetry Foundation survey, the National Endowment for the Arts conducted its own survey on reading. It does not hold out very good prospects for nonreaders. And it does not take into account just how much text is devoured online — surely the equivalent of many books — which as we know is still not the equivalent of a single particular text. And this is the swift decline they could measure: the deep, unrivaled pleasure of deep reading.

Just before the wiring and then the wireless changed everything, I attempted to make the argument for slow being better, old being good, quiet being required. I conclusively lost that case. I cannot make anything stop moving. I cannot convince the young that the old are good when they (the young) are salivating over their inheritance, not because they think they are entitled, but because they think they'll be eating dirt. Dirty dirt at that. Nor can I put the earth noise on pause. I have to keep coming back to the word being carved into poetry as something that in and of itself puts a much-needed, no, a necessary drag on a single construal; that retrieves; that accumulates density even as it accelerates.

Even so, poetry gestures toward silence as it speaks and casts its stillness about us. There is, however, the threat of total, full-time, all-over silence. Death clings to poetry. It brings back the taste of ashes. It directs you to the forehock. Religion consoles; many believe it cleanses. Poetry faces the end without obfuscation. But much is to be said for "going down fighting."

Poets do not have the answer. They say what they see. They take their own pulse. They stay up thinking of lines of poetry that they might use.

I say, teach your kids to read.

Poetry's twin desiderata: to speak once and for all, to forever hold its peace. Like the old man said, "Do I contradict myself? Very well then I contradict myself." A hundred years later John Ashbery murmured, "I thought that if I could put it all down, that would be one way. [But] to leave it all out would be another, and truer, way." A blank page can serve as one poem, as close to perfect as one poem may come. It cannot serve as poetry.

Changing the name won't help any more than switching parties that are already pretty freaking interchangeable.

I am not bent on the preservation of the genre in anything approximating a pure form. (It's a poem if I say it is.) Yet I am not convinced poems, novels, plays have exhausted their own stock-in-trade. I do not think the genres persist, to the degree that they do, just to conform to marketing requirements. Regardless of identifiable practice, no crossover, hybrid, blended, or the dissolution of taxonomies will bring the readers around.

When has poetry not availed itself of everything from full-frontal sex to crackpot economics. When has it not worked every effect known to literature, especially the longer its history and the more extended its compositions. When has the uncategorizable not justly been called poetry. I say, when it begins to stink. At the stinking point, all writing should retreat to its own smelly corner—as bad poetry, bad fiction, bad theater, bad meat. Poetry should not be the default for every writer's mess. Otherwise, it is a poem if I say it is.

I quickly poll a few of my contemporaries as to why poetry matters more now than when it mattered less than before: "It prevents us from living a fixed life… a life of stasis," Jenny Boully suggests: "Now, more than ever, when the world seems to be experiencing so much strife because of beliefs that are rooted in a fixed worldview, we need poems to remind us what it is to be this or that, to feel joy or sadness, to marvel at our physical universe." Arthur Sze wrote, "Poetry matters more than ever before, because we are more challenged than ever before. Poetry is the essential language that, endlessly branching, enables us to live deeply and envision what matters most…. Poetry dissolves boundaries—it is the finite that puts us in touch with the infinite—and, as languages and species vanish every day, it is a crucial vehicle by which we apprehend the urgency and precarious splendor of existence." And Ben Lerner: "The scarcer the spaces for this formal exercise, the less we are asked to ask ourselves to relate part to whole, the SUV to the dirty war, the more desperately important such spaces become…. The ideal poem and Fox News are opposites. The former enlists your participation, teaches you to see patterns, while the latter is divided into categories… whose boundaries guarantee their emptiness…. Maybe a culture that attends to poetry is in a better position to unfix the language from the ruinous project of concealing the forms we live by." And Forrest Gander: "Because in a time of spectacle, poetry is the anti-spectacle, the wormhole through silence into the interior rich with nuance, with feeling sparked by intuition and attentiveness… the place of our deeper transformations and renewals." And Cole Swensen, "I think of endangered species…. [Poetry is] an entire way of thinking, and the less we have of it in the world, the less variety in thinking there is around—and it seems we need continued broadening of thought modes, never narrowing." And from Jane Miller, "Poetry has given me life. Then I think, how maudlin, then I think, how sane." Maybe Walmart doesn't rule.

The poets lock themselves in and work off-the-clock. Of their own volition. They leave lines lying around the break rooms. Lines of their own making.

Everyone I ask sounds a note of urgency if not emergency. We must find the words, we must put them down, we must order them, we must resuscitate neglected terms, discover new forms; we must scrawl on the walls in our own waste if we have to, but mostly in cyberspace, which provides a surface without end.

"There is disequilibrium between ourselves and the world that nothing restores to balance but poetry," writes Brenda Hillman. The attention it demands ensures that "the qualities of individual words and their relationships to one another are what matters.... Loving words is a way of staying interested... Poetry allows the mind to come into contact with the impossible oddness of everything."

The world at risk is the meaning of words. The felicitously manifold meanings of words. And if meaning itself be mangled beyond recognition... Are you next of kin? Are you next?

I say, teach your kids to read poetry.

Poetry abhors the lie. The lies we are told, they pile up, they become truth by virtue of the heap. By their volume. By virtue of constant recapitulation. Many things we absolutely knew to be true were, by dint of being spoken in isolation, delivered in silent space, sifted through the archaeology of lies to the bottom. There is no room to breathe on the bottom.

Poetry digs through. Its castings make some growth possible even on contaminated ground. Though forced to make do with shrinking day-length, though forced to go the worm's way, poetry ensures new shoots. It could be that an international vault will have to be established for poetry, to ensure the renewal of the greatest variety of voices, of lines capable of challenging the uniformity of thought. The vault that must by definition of its mission reject the Walmart cheer. Spring clings to poetry. It brings forth possibility, "the greatest good."

That the poems we snatch from the language must bear the habit of our thinking.

That their arrangement strengthens the authority on which each separate line is laid.

That they extend the line into perpetuity.

That they enlarge the circle.

That they awaken the dreamer. That they awaken the schemer.

That they rectify the names.

That they draw not conclusions but further qualify doubt.

That they avail themselves of the shrapnel of everything: the disappearance of cork trees and coral, the destroyed center of Ramadi, the shape of buildings to come, the pearness of pears.

That they clear the air.

That they keep a big-box sense of humor at the ready (like an ax in a glass case).

That they bring the ship nearer to its longing.

That they resensitize the surface of things.

That they resonate in the bowels.

That they will not stand alone.

This is our mind. Our language. Our light. Our word. Our bond.

In the world.

Jean Valentine, Abridged

When I read Jean Valentine's poems I fill up with questions, flow over with emotion. I cease, in some way, to think. At least the din of thinking dies back. Instead: "To be there; to listen; not invade…. / Not to invade Wait, here, in the quiet." A great silence is anterior to what gets said, so that what is said must, by necessity, be put down, expressed.

+ + +

It is not that the writing is hermetic; in fact, I believe its entire pitch and purpose is openness. I grasp that the whole life — of loving and losing, erring and righting, reading and thinking, saying and seeing — is faithfully recorded, word for word, and submerged under each elliptic dot. She is "shy of words but desperately true to them," wrote Seamus Heaney. "Looking into a Jean Valentine poem is like looking into a lake," wrote Adrienne Rich. I think I see what Valentine sees: her own outline and what has settled below. But I am wary of describing it.

Poetry was.
Poetry is.
Poetry will be.

Providing it avoids its own stasis—which, I notice, it does—it may be *the* future, given how unfulfilling and ruinous many human endeavors are, how swiftly discarded almost any given set of long-acquired skills. Henry Miller wrote something along the lines of the biggest terror of the one who mucks out the stalls is a world without horses. *Ergo* if poetry goes and horses go, in either order, who is going to deal with all the muck. Because muck there will be, horse or no horse; without poetry, much more muck.

Bookburn

Speaking personally, to read or not to read is like asking to starve or not to starve. I am still attached to the illusion that I can lay a hand on a book and feel its heat.

Spring & All

The Great War is barely in the background. The fatal flu pandemic fills the void, concentrating on the young and healthy. This weird little book is brought into the world the same month as the Munich Beer Hall Putsch, Hitler's first major drive to seize control. Among artists and writers, the urge for renewal is gaining ground in the aftermath of monstrous destruction, in the bud of worse to come. It is boggling that so much hearty artistic innovation has commenced to proliferate and thrive. Do or die. Those who can, do. Even the wreckage of Europe is tempting to the young, creative, contrary, and restless. One American writer stays put, finishes school, starts a medical practice. One American writer sticks around to catch the babies.

In a Word,
a World

Although I take a special pleasure in compounds, whether or not they have been duly authorized—*silverback, deepstep, lovegreen, pothead, eyestring, closeburn, shirttail, boneman, wristwatch*—no words please me so much as the one- or two-syllable noun. It appears at its best left unaccompanied by an article. At its best, shed of adjective. Whether it is singular or plural matters. I prefer *hours* to *hour* and *roads* to *road; hills* to *hill, faces* to *face,* but also *fish* to *fishes* and *tooth* to *teeth.* Does it matter whether I know the reason. Or that I can but vaguely supply one. Probably, but the reasons hop around, and seem purely personal. Writing is choosing. Choosing is decision-making. Decisions among word choices are among the most delectable of the whole writing experience. They may be accidental, they may be serendipitous. Never arbitrary. Decisions are being made. Even when subliminal. An accurate computation of the decisions involved in composing a poem of three–five lines would be an Oulipian challenge. I like the weight, I like the lilt, I like the scene. I don't like the *s* here but do not mind it there. I like the noun to situate hue. A gourd is gourd-colored. It's extra if its sound value complements its substance, say, for example, *hock.* (Whereas *God* is just very odd.) And optimal when much of its *-ness*–ness as possible is thought held in its common name. On the other hand, there's an off-kiltering pleasure in discovering that words do not mean what you might think they would: *debridement,* for instance; *adumbrate, disinterest, enervate,* and *nonplussed* are frequent tripper-uppers.

Spring & All

Spring and All was reprinted in Dijon, by the same Darantiere who had printed *Ulysses* the year before; so the printer, at least, was already familiar with the oddities the English language could bear. Robert McAlmon's Paris-based Contact Publishing Company issued Williams's manifesto-of-sorts in an edition of 300, most of which went undistributed. The year before, 1922, was high tide in poetry: *Duino Elegies, Trilce,* and *The Waste Land.* The last was a head-blow to William Carlos Williams. He had more or less absorbed the concussion of "Prufrock" and sounded off on it in his prologue to *Kora in Hell.* He had recalibrated and redoubled to the task of staking out the new word for the not-so-new-anymore world. Then came *The Waste Land,* all tricked out with Sanskrit and Latin ornaments. The impact was as useful as it was painful. *Whap.* Now Williams knew what he was opposing; now he could move in the direction he wanted to go—forward—in his "small (or large) machine made of words." For Williams, poetry was meant to be in motion. He willed himself ready: "How easy to slip / into the old mode, how hard to / cling firmly to the advance—"

+ + +

Williams epitomized the prepared observer. A watcher, a listener. Goat stubborn. Feet-in-the-soil independent. He could write whatever, whenever, and as he damn well pleased. William Carlos Williams was the embodiment of values Americans touted but seemed capable of expressing only in "isolate flecks." With an English father and Puerto Rican mother, there was no compelling incentive to become an expat. He would embrace the contrary impulse. Like his fellow New Jerseyan, Whitman, his apostrophe was to the future, but he hankered for contact here and now. The charge of this writing was change. His own personal epic and constantly shifting landscape were just on the other side of the parlor window, the whole procession. Like Whitman, he would gradually come to a great human understanding, an apprehension that eluded a number of his peers.

The not knowing
whether what you've set down is any good

You don't, you never know, as his lordliness the besotted John Berryman told an ingenue, the parson's son W.S. Merwin. If you have to know, don't write. Frankly, if you are easily satisfied with your efforts, it is probably too facile a task for you. If it does not push and pull you to the frontiers of what you know, and then on to where the really good stuff — all that you do not know — is, you need a more strenuous challenge. Something that really blows your knees out. The painter Ed Ruscha is reported by Dave Hickey to have claimed, "Bad art is 'Wow! Huh?' Good art is 'Huh? Wow!'" That pretty much hits the spot for me.

Poetry is hard to abuse except by writing it poorly, and then the damage, face it, is finite.

Hold Still, Lion

In post–World War II America there were several loosely affiliated, overlapping strands of poets who began publishing—poets rejecting the epistemological and anglophile models of W.H. Auden and T.S. Eliot. They were known variously as the New York School, the San Francisco Renaissance, the Beats, and the Black Mountain poets. They came up on the heels of Ezra Pound and William Carlos Williams, and along the spur of the Objectivists, aka Zukofsky, Reznikoff, Niedecker, et al. Robert Creeley was the bridge. He distributed the differences and sounded parallel concerns. He began corresponding with Pound and Williams in 1949. He and John Ashbery were seated two desks apart at Harvard. In Majorca, his Divers Press published Robert Duncan and Paul Blackburn. He typed Allen Ginsberg's *Howl,* which was then mimeographed in an edition of twenty-five. At the now legendary and gone Black Mountain College, he studied with Charles Olson and "earned" his successorship. At Black Mountain Creeley edited the *Black Mountain Review* (initially from Majorca) and picked up the degree he had managed not to complete at Harvard. Over the years he would edit works of Charles Olson and George Oppen (and Robert Burns and Walt Whitman), as well as anthologies of new American writing. His correspondence was carried on at a rate and level not to be believed. The Olson/Creeley letters alone consume ten volumes (if e-mail had been available to those two the number of volumes might have been squared). He wrote tense stories and a superb short novel along with scores of word-perfect essays. Overall he published in the vicinity of seventy books. Checking a familiar book site, 227 titles are instantly identified with his name. His collaborations with artists including Francesco Clemente, Elsa Dorfman, Sol LeWitt, R.B. Kitaj, and Susan Rothenberg were the occasion of fine-edition books and traveling exhibitions. His collaborations with musicians such as Steve Lacy and Steve Swallow were performed for packed, hip audiences and are featured on numerous recordings. He could and did fill Albert

Hall, but he had no qualms about reading to a crowd of four. No qualms, either, about talking extemporaneously in lieu of giving the promoted reading. He was not there to accommodate anyone's prepackaged expectations — he was there to discover the direction of his own thinking. And in that lies, as he often quoted William Carlos Williams, the profundity.

Hold Still, Lion

When I wrote to poet Rosmarie Waldrop (who was out of the country at the time), regarding Robert Creeley's death, she responded, "It is the end of a world."

René Char asked, What can we do to bring
the ship nearer to its longing?

That is a fine, a beautiful question. Think of this effort with a pinch of mystery, won't you. A vein of melancholy. Elegance even; even if you are a realist, which vexes my own perspective (alongside melancholy), it is an ever-unfolding exploration. "What must we do to get to the school of dreams," asks Hélène Cixous, posing it as the most urgent of questions.

Between great hails to the imagination and salvos of opprobrium, William Carlos Williams set one sharp-edged poem after another into the composition of an unframed original. So the one who did not cast off his roots chose the oldest trope in the book, SPRING, to push and pull American poetry into the present tense. Not before he had initiated a willful number of false starts, cranking up anticipation and repeatedly sabotaging expectations. Not before the hectored reader was fetched up "by the road to the contagious hospital," only then would the first glimpse of grass and "the stiff curl of wildcarrot leaf" be permitted — at the precise point at which every stick in the refuse emerged particular. *Terrifying,* as Robert Creeley was given to say.

Nuptials & Violence

There is a word, *meuse,* whose obsolete meaning is the form of an animal left by its lying, particularly a hare and other creatures of game. It is imagined that all of the world bears our mark, holds our form, and that the land is reminiscent in detail of all that ever came of its issue, was built on its foundation, or came to great harm on its surface. I met a French poet who lives on the edge of a silent land. Somme, 1916: estimated casualties, over one million. Somme, Celtic in origin, for "tranquility."

Jane Miller applies her considerable lyric stamina to the paragraph. Not a journal, not a narrative — *these outpourings,* she says at one point, but they are much more formal and unsparing than the word conveys. *Pure crying,* she says, but the tears come in shifts and are dried by sustained commentary on their source, even on their comparative insignificance, yet individuated as they must be. Four discrete lyrics are in position to wick off any excess in the prose.

The mother soils herself and the daughter bathes her with a warm washcloth. The lover leaves and the poet pukes a divine meal in a divine hotel room. Don't empty your suitcase yet, Gentle Reader — there's a funeral, a two-stringed instrument with the scroll of a horse's head, a brief treatise on owls, a little subversive music to foil the junta — whole new pathways articulating their coursings to and from the heart until the last syllable sings itself out. What a splendid testament to the ill fortunes of love.

Purgatorio

In a national crisis, not everyone goes into exile; indeed, not everyone, Zurita included, has the option. Nor does everyone else disappear or die or meld with the silent majority. Neither is anyone spared. Thus, along with a cadre of others opposed to Pinochet, the former student, young father, and husband was allotted his defining, historical moment. Otherwise he might have completed his engineering studies, written poetry on the side, and pursued an industrious, if less catastrophic, ruminating and preoccupied life.

+ + +

Perforce, Zurita created a groundbreaking document of Chile's most anguished chapter in the twentieth century. *Purgatorio* opens with the author admitting that his friends think he, having disfigured his own face, might not be quite right. Then, a photo of his bandaged cheek with the text below, *EGO SUM;* and then: "My name is Rachel," and the text, *QUI SUM,* introducing the first of the speaker's starkly differing identities.

+ + +

Already have we crossed a frontier where things are not what they seem, people are not who they claim to be. The destination is not paradise, but the beach of purgatory, Chile's Atacama, some part of which climatologists have designated *absolute desert.* Atacama, driest place on Earth, site of the ultimate challenge to conjure a language again: the brilliant, blinding blank page. Atacama, a place from which the broken column, the fleeing herd, the abandoned Christ, Zurita and friends can at least cry out: *eli eli,* moo, *eli eli,* bleat, *eli eli.* Chile's landscape is just dramatic enough for the extremities of Zurita's expression.

+ + +

Midway along the unguided path of *Purgatorio* a handwritten letter, from a psychologist, is inserted into the poem, a diagnosis of epileptic psychosis. The patient's name, Raúl Zurita, has been scratched out, replaced by Violeta, scratched out, replaced by Sweet Beatriz, scratched out, and so on. In the final pages, a series of encephalograms record the persistent sputterings of a normal mind under distressed conditions. To a significant degree, Zurita's future would be behind him by the end of the Pinochet era. But he would still have to propose a paradise.

During the Composition of
Rising, Falling, Hovering

(a personal document of the war, of Mexico, and of an American family's halting progress)

She worked in the negative. She worked against herself. Always. If she were to get the hang of something, she took it as a sign to try something another way, e.g., eliminate punctuation so as to face the bare ground on which the words are affixed. Learn where the silence is freighted, where it secures an emptiness, where it marks the spot, and where it stands in for syntax. The line responds to punctuation's absence — flush left, indent, hit tab, and distribute across the page with caesuras. These are not radical maneuvers, but it takes (at least for some) a great deal of force to push the mule over a very short distance. One is taking new stock of breath, cadence, phrasing. One is looking for an alternate route.

That is one way. The other way is to go at it the same as before. If it worked then, why not now. Just as legitimate. The possibility exists that it is the most assured way of really getting down in there. It could be termed *repeating oneself*. But even that is harder to do than one would have thought except when unintentional. Then it is just unfortunate. It is termed *slipping*. But making a calculated effort to repeat tended to bring her to the exact same spot as before — the spot where access was sealed off. If she had to come back to the sealed-off area again and again, at least she could alter the course. At the wheel, even, driving them home, she made him crazy, taking so many routes. So inefficient, such a waste of time, when the goal was to get there — to, in fact, be there.

The buildup to the war, our XXX-rated creepshow, was underway. Its inevitability came with the spoiled election of 2000. In the wake of the September attacks, the countdown could proceed at an accelerated pace and in public view, because now the public would have to pay both in dollars and blood.

+ + +

The family went to Mexico. They were often going to Mexico for one reason or another. Or no reason. Mexico beckoned; they went. Growing up, the Rio Grande was the only national border her body passed over. In her early twenties, she took an unplanned trip to the Yucatán, traveling through the peninsula on second-class buses with her college roommate — no itinerary, no luggage, no money: just go go go. From a humid colonial hotel in Mérida to a freezing, dilapidated compound in San Cristóbal. And some years after that, a fellowship from the NEA prompted her to quit her job at the Poetry Center and move with her then-boyfriend to Guanajuato. He had finished his graduate degree and was working at the methadone clinic. They both quit. First they drove from San Francisco to her family home in Arkansas. They left his car in her parents' driveway, which means they had followed each other from California, a long-distance fact she had all but forgotten. Her father was so alarmed by the *US OUT OF EL SALVADOR* bumper sticker on her car that he scraped it off while they slept. He was afraid they would be jumped in Arkansas or strung up in Texas before they ever saw the crazy blue skies of Mexico. She had an extra sticker in her glove compartment and promptly replaced the one he had removed. It was luck that they had chosen to take her car and not her boyfriend's: hers used leaded gas, though they weren't cognizant of this advantage beforehand. When they crossed the border, they had to pay the border guard a *mordida*. It did not bode well for how they were going to negotiate in-country, but "the bite" was never exacted again. She remembered her then-boyfriend musing, *Hmmm, things are in a different language over here,* and so they were, and on they went over the pitted, shoulderless highway. Cows soaking up the heat off the asphalt in the evening and goats tinkling across by day. The first night they backed the station wagon up against a crumbling wall and checked into a dirty, windowless room in San Luis Potosí, an experience they never needed to repeat, staying in cheap, lovely hotels in many pueblos to come. They thought they were going to take up residence in Guanajuato, a random destination, but when they slid down the hill into the city on failing brakes, they had a change of heart and returned to Dolores Hidalgo, the tranquil, historic town they passed through en route to the state's capital.

He was diligent about studying Spanish. He collected poetry by Mexican women to translate. She opted out, becoming more or less de-languaged. They lived in a second-story apartment of the Vasquez family home, typing away at an unsalvageable jumble of material. They stayed half as long as they'd planned because he, with no spleen to defend himself, became too sick to stay longer. Still, whenever an opportunity arose in the years hence, they were back. Only once did they stop in Dolores Hidalgo. They learned that Señor Vasquez, their landlord, was still living; yet they shrank from going to see him. Too much time had passed, and they were too disappointed in the town's metamorphosis into a honking, clogged commercial center.

Soon after second Gulf War commenced, she was at the airport again. It was late — one delay begat another. She saw Senator Chafee waiting for a flight back to Washington, and approached him to thank him, the lone Republican voting nay. He said he had just attended a hockey game, and that the Canadian team had booed the U.S. team. She told him what she had heard and what she had seen in Mexico — the flower vendors in the Alameda spelling out their protest with their *flores*, NO A LA GUERRA Y SI A LA PAZ; the taxis in a miles-long queue flying pennants for peace; the candlelit vigils in the courtyards of churches, the editorials, effigies, and graffiti. The senator said he was not going to be turned around. She wanted her poem to show the range of opposition. She did not want to be anecdotal. Often lineation just does not bear up. Instead, she tried applying more pressure to passages that asserted themselves as prose.

The teenage years were very hard on their intense trinity. The desperate crucible of an American family, tense and isolate and confused, a barely survivable unit. They rocked on through. The son's last summer of high school, they sent him to Mexico to learn Spanish. He did not learn the language, but he learned to move around on his own. They sent him to the heart of Mexico to learn Spanish, and within hours of his arrival he was on a bus to Zihuatanejo, hundreds of miles from the language school.

Pictures Never Taken but Received

Photographs are a writing of the light. *Photos graphein.* Or in some instances *photos graphone.* I can hear them. Some say, (you) be careful. Be afraid. Love. Be true. Gnaw. Be brave. Clot. Be real. Scream. Hush. Listen. Womb. Sleep now. "Be still. The Hanging Gardens were a dream." Some engage only the silent aftermath. The relationship of poetry to silence is as involved as that of photography's. In photography, silence is a given and an effect. In poetry it is a state of mind and an effect. Several hundred amplified color pictures just arrived in my dropbox absorbing and scattering and monopolizing the light. Perhaps the greater responsibility lies with poetry, in any engagement with photography (rather than vice versa), to sort through the inaudible signals before speaking up.

On a wall in Whitechapel I saw it written:
I propose to keep looking. *I propose*
we all keep looking. I propose
it is an unyielding imperative for the poet to do so.

In a Word,
a World

I also admit a weakness for prefixes over suffixes, *un-* in particular because I favor the negative: *unbegotten, unforgiven, unhorsed.* Whereas *-ism*s are too ideological and *-itis*es too pathological. Some words should be said more than once for their effect, *river river.* Said once, it quickly shivers and stops. Seconded, it begins to flow. A word is chosen and put into position, for particular effect. It is tantamount to hauling a big rock, carrying it a great distance, and setting it down, only to realize it should not be occupying that spot in this circumstance. It is dead on arrival but you barely have the reserves to move it again. Although if not moved, and best before darkness spreads, it will create a hole commensurate with its heft, and it will encroach on the tender shoots of words nearby. If, however, it was the exact word you wanted and rightly lodged, the satisfaction is granted, on-the-spot, so to speak. And the entire surround is enhanced. Then, there is its commonly attendant ability to convert its stationariness into action. One can truck on over to that enormous rock and rock it out of the hole it is beginning to create for itself. I rock, you rock, one trucks.

Jean Valentine, Abridged

The poems stay resolutely strange. When I say the writing is strange, I mean the writing resides on the positive side of the strangeness axis. She writes "strangely" with painful intimacy. Told, "but you couldn't have been different / from the way you were," discloses, "but I *would* to have been different." The reader can guess at the failures that lie under that admission, alluded to here and there; she cannot but esteem the formality ("I *would* to have been different") whereby it is tendered. Emotion is never dodged, only the details. The reader is led to a private space, and left there by herself, to contemplate her own reprehensible acts.

+ + +

The poet keeps her devotions. Catholic, Buddhist, Hindu, Gnostic, Jungian? She lights candles, gets on her knees, throws the *I Ching*, writes down her dreams, sees a therapist. Open, I say: she is mindfully open. A dreamer. A quiet, wide-awake child writing a letter to an imaginary friend.

Spring & All

From page one, Dr. Williams lurches into an exchange with his imaginary critics. In lieu of titles or subtitles or headings, he spoofs the typographical stunts of the times, using both Arabic and Roman "chapter" numbers to fence off units of poetry and prose, completely out of sequence. Chapter XIII appears upside down. The effect creates a minor distraction, albeit intentional, but it is the abrupt shifting, cutting, and swerving that prevent the reader from ever relaxing into the text. The suspense of the performance is carried all the way to "the edge of the petal." Does love wait there? Will spring ever come? Who is Kiki — the nurse, the artist's model, the waif in the long-running play? Will the doctor please elucidate what he christens *imagination*. What does J.P. Morgan have to do with anything except what new money can buy: old masters. What does it mean to be "drunk with goats or pavements"? Country or city? Who else but Williams would grasp that the place to get the latest news about the weather and the last word on death is the barbershop? Who else cared what the barber thought? And when the whole atavistic American scene gets intolerable, would anyone be there to drive the car? *Tranquilly Titicaca* indeed.

+ + +

The prose is a working-through, hot with argument, loud with opinion. The overall form is a grand improvisation. Here a little rapture on the possible; here a riff on Shakespeare, on Poe, on Anatole France. The poetry was struck in one sitting, executed with what Hugh Kenner called Williams's "great technical perception." Here an ekphrastic poem of a painting by Juan Gris; here a homage to le jazz hot, le jazz cool; here a snapshot of what he saw through the windshield, or notations scribbled onto a prescription pad. References ladled out of the "skyscraper soup" of industry, advertising, local speech—all the while spring itself was stiffly becoming manifest.

Are we still seers and dreamers

I would say so, but seeing and dreaming are not exactly held at a premium, and the tempo of the day makes it very hard to make what you see stand still long enough for you to articulate, makes the dreams harder to clarify. Frank O'Hara said poetry is as useful as a machine. He didn't feel the need to justify his statement. Allen Grossman called poetry "the historical enemy of human forgetfulness, the historical agent... against the obliterative powers of the world." I heard Heather McHugh tell an audience there are two points in life for which poetry is an absolute necessity: the point of love and the point of death. There are numerous ways to posit its significance, none of them very helpful, in the database. Ron Silliman wrote that the one function that could not be taken away from poetry is that it is the art of language without limit. We are still, as Wordsworth was, trying to "see into the life of things." Testimonials abound. It would not be my personal choice to live in a world without poetry. I think I have already glimpsed that world. It is just not rufus.

The Book We Hold in Common

Art critic Peter Schjeldahl (a once-upon-a-time poet) wrote, "Painting survives on a case-by-case basis, its successes amounting to special exemptions from a verdict of history." This is a slimmed-down version of what might lie ahead for poetry. There is a communal component to poetry as it is currently practiced, advanced, and transmitted which makes me think the case-by-case trial would turn poetry into a very destructive effort, poet against poet, eye against eye; soon everybody blind.

(Peter Schjeldahl was born in Fargo. Which explains exactly what? His surname.)

The Book That Brenda Wrote

One of the most captivating books of poetry I have read in recent years is Brenda Hillman's *Seasonal Works with Letters On Fire,* the fourth in her quartet based on the fundamental Greek elements, to which she has determined to add a fifth, wood. Unique even to Hillman, who is on the qui vive for "the impossible oddness of everything." To describe it would be to fail to describe it; so this is a bid to lay in a track about the effect of its company.

To my way of reading, Hillman has always been an idiosyncratic writer, always on her own adventure, increasingly engaged with the shape of her poetry — the shape of poetry in general, both formally and exigently, in relation to its actual environment. With this title she has emptied the contents of her big purse, which includes her home library, her workaday life, her childhood, her family, her gnostic self, her warrior self, her brainy self, her sumptuous, seasonal self — all intensified by a fervent hunger and thirst for the protection and preservation of Earth and its earthlings. Out of which, BH's Great Array. Small wonder when she focused on fire with the mother tongue of poetry, delivered into the most unwelcome sectors, she paused just long enough to ask herself, "Pointless? Maybe its points are moving, as in a fire."

Even her justified anger bears a trace of bounty. The animated light of her fury inspires one to get up and stomp. She is lightning "the sea shines purple in." With a seed bomb of words, she takes on *the system* (a term that has come to sound almost endearing), without once turning her back on lyrical splendor.

What looms now is ever more anonymous and unresponsive than any high-ranking, clanking, rusty Systemizers could devise. It is the inhuman.

My American Scrawl

Poetry requires movement in its direction, faith in its persistence, receptivity to its fundamental worthwhileness. Within its unanesthetized chambers there is quite a commotion going on. Choices have to be made with respect to every mark. Not every mistake should be erased. Nor shall the unintelligible be left out. Order is there to be macheted from the tangles of words. Results are impossible to measure. A clearing is drawn around the perimeter as if by a crooked stick with a crooked nail on the end.

(I remain haunted by the poem Amina Massey wrote whose title that I cannot recall came from a language I cannot recall, a language no longer spoken, and means to love for the last time.*)*

In a Word,
a World

I love the nouns of a time in a place, where a sack once was a poke and native skag
was junk glass not junk and junk was just junk not smack and smack entailed
eating with your mouth open, and an Egyptian one-eye was an egg, sunny-side
up, and a nation sack was a flannel amulet, worn only by women, to be touched
only by women, especially around Memphis. Red sacks for love and green for
money. Of course the qualifying adjective *nation* does exercise an otherwise
uneventful noun.

Nuptials & Violence

Deborah's next-door neighbor, Kenneth Holditch, a Tennessee Williams scholar who has long been enthroned in the Marigny, officiated.

A small park in front of the house lies in a daytime soundtrack of children, dogs, and airborne insects. By nine the park is locked; the first set is warming up at the Spotted Cat. The trombonist takes it out on the sidewalk to loosen his slide.

Some nights, the chop of helicopter blades makes talking on the phone undoable.

A cornucopia of clouds drifts over Angola.

The wedding march, "Sexual Healing" by Marvin Gaye, was performed by the Hot 8 Brass Band, three of whose members have been killed by men and children wielding guns: seventeen-year-old trumpet player Jacob Johnson was shot execution-style in his home; trombone player Joe Williams was shot by the police (as a teen, Mr. Williams along with his brothers and sisters witnessed the shooting death of his mother by his father at the dinner table). Most recently the band lost snare drummer Dinerral Shavers, whose accused murderer was acquitted and later charged with attempted murder for a shooting following his release. The alleged shooter was seventeen at the time of the prior charge. A million-dollar bail has been set for David Bonds, the accused, nineteen. Now he is officially a man.

During the Composition of
Rising, Falling, Hovering (*cont.*)

When another war is decided, apocalyptic fears proliferate. The family was in Oaxaca City the night the U.S. started dropping its bombs on Baghdad. The next morning the front pages were posted on the partitions of the periodical stands and on stucco walls alongside nearly psychotropic cascades of bougainvillea. And one was always face-to-face with a television in a lobby or in the open-air cafés, tiendas, and cantinas. She didn't meet anyone in Mexico from any profession, any trade, who believed the war was justified. Didn't encounter anyone who believed the president was telling the truth about why this had to be done. BÁRBARO ATAQUE was one headline. Befriending Americans and believing the American government operated with contempt for the rest of the world were still givens. Their southern neighbors were annealed not only to the U.S. modus operandi but also to their own government's ubiquitous corruption—the real differential was in the scale of state-sponsored depredation.

The marriage was strained by the difficulties they were having with their son. The son's opposition had a momentum and a course of its own. No one was in control. But no one was willing to cry Tío.

She did a lot of reading about Mexico. Reading in and around a subject—books suggested by other books—was a compulsion whether it qualified as research. Her book of books, during the composition of the first half of her long poem, was a short memoir about traveling through the Tierra Caliente in 1951, *Where the Strange Roads Go Down*. She wrung that reading into a single skinny passage. The poem did not have a plot as such, it was episodic, and different parties were brought in without firm respect for logic. Juxtaposition was a strategy with which she was comfortable.

She spent a month on her own in a bungalow in Marfa, Texas, often driving around in a rental car near the border—picking up stories of much earlier raids and massacres, of drug deals, illegal crossings, the border patrol and vigilantes. She persuaded her friend Deborah Luster to come out for a week. Deborah photographed the ruin of a barracks where Esequiel Hernández Jr., a U.S. citizen herding goats after school, was shot by U.S. marines. It pretty much destroyed the small border community. The Hernández family withdrew; the goat-cheese collective dissolved. And it wasn't long before the schools consolidated, forcing the local kids to commute a distance from Redford. (Tommy Lee Jones used the boy's murder as part of the storyline for a much-overlooked 2005 release, *The Three Burials of Melquiades Estrada*.) The marines were pulled off of drug enforcement on the border after the death of the Hernández boy, but the dirty deed was done. On the wall beside Esequiel's bed was a marine recruitment poster. The marine shooter was Mexican American. She could not work in these black ironies, but the lethal consequences of an illegal crossing are imagined near the end of the first half of the poem.

She wrote it, then added *to be cont.*, because she had a sense that she was not finished. She added it because it pleased her to put an old convention back into service. She added *to be cont.*, because whether she wrote more or not, nothing was resolved, nothing was resolved. Another year passed, longer, between the poem's first part and its continuation.

The war insinuated itself everywhere. She read the reports and the obituaries obsessively. She said to herself that she would set her hair on fire before they would get her firstborn, her only one. At the time, they rarely exchanged a civil word. And of course, the draft did not exist to force the hair-burning issue. It was obvious who was being enlisted, who shipping out. Who being maimed, who killed; whose mothers were being given the folded flags. Not the college-bound, not even the dicey kids such as her own, who were much more attracted to the brink than the expected track. And it didn't seem to take a New York minute before the government and the popular media had demonized the general population of Iraq into utterly nonhuman status. How does that work? We are real, they are not! The destruction would be totalizing. And the profit for the profiteers, beyond belief. It didn't seem to take any time to kick out enough acceptance of the war for elected and installed officials and high-level appointees to be cowed into support when they weren't already thumping their tails and jabbing their fingers in the faces of the resistant and the resisters. *Impacto e intimidación*. Bring it on.

Was it not incumbent on all who opposed the war to protest by whatever means available to them. Poetry never seems up to the task. Poetry is always up for more than she gave it credit. But picking the words to pin to the unflagging fury the regime inspired, building the frame to ensure the word could weather that perilous emotion — it was one of those by-hook-or-crook courses of movement. She was at a juncture in her life where she was tumultuously involved with her immediate family + Mexico offered a fertile, entangled place in which her thoughts could explore her thoughts + a close friend, a Mexican poet, had a bad diagnosis. They went back — this time to Cuernavaca. A year before, they had gone to celebrate their friend's birthday; now they were helping her fill a few chilly evenings while her husband attended a conference in Asia.

Any visit to that particular city put one back in mind of one of the twentieth century's more harrowing English-language novels, *Under the Volcano*. To this day she credited it with two critical life decisions: not to become a novelist (since the book she would have wanted to write but could not and need not was, in fact, written) and not to become a dedicated dissolute (since she would surely never write a legible word if she took the plunge down that ravine). In the meantime, the war was of course worsening. The British medical magazine *The Lancet* published death tolls of 665,000, many times over what the major U.S. media was putting on its front pages and in its fifteen-second broadcasts. The U.S. government pooh-poohed any assessments that it did not itself generate, minimizing the humanitarian crisis while continuing to manufacture a glorious outcome.

She submitted to one of those page-turning binges of which she retained next to nothing, reading William H. Prescott's theatrically wrought *History of the Conquest of Mexico*. The blind scholar, who never actually went to Mexico, developed a vivid thesis of a titanic struggle between Montezuma and Cortés. It was riveting, but left her somewhat enervated. She did not aspire to such scope or bombast in her poem, but she could, instead, intensify the focus of her limited experience. Sometimes the lines would be chiseled to the size of what she might plausibly see, such as a graveside service from her bedroom (though she invented the one of which she wrote); or she'd use a rant that tore off from her grey matter after reading the day's events.

And something about reading the news, about the newspaper itself (though she read a fair amount online), the material object of a daily, provided a loose substratum: obituaries, squibs, sidebars, stock phrases, the juxtaposition of the mundane and the tragic, a barrage of disconnected yet weirdly interdependent stories — set against the ongoing minidrama of their own lives playing out in a dappled, green town in New England. How to twine one's ethical lens with one's somewhat more antiseptic conditioning to write outside the limits of conviction. Arthur Sze: "The mind craves to make something perdurable / out of something as tenuous as candlelight, / something that becomes more and more itself / through vicissitude."

The process was painstaking—spread out over several years and geographies—the more so because it was lived-in; because it was temperamental by dint of its sources; because one can imagine more readily obstacles that do not exist than one can imagine apertures that do; because poetry, alas, makes nothing happen. In the end, she was more satisfied than she expected to be since the process was so protracted and procured so little solace. She was startled that she could not retrace her steps except in the form of a submerged, third-person narrative. More than once, she had sat at the computer and read the entire poem aloud, and could not herself figure out exactly how she had created certain passages, only that she felt a gnashing need that she could not begin to meet but could address in stops and starts. A rhythm never asserted itself; the pattern was tessellated at best, but the individual words were very insistent. They had to be just so, and they had to be positioned here and here. She meant every solitary, begged, borrowed, stolen, and conjured phoneme. Other accounts that she had read of individuals making something that hadn't quite been there before had unrolled in like manner.

Hold Still, Lion

With the 1962 publication of *For Love*, Robert Creeley became a world poet, an icon, albeit in the American grain. From Buffalo, poet Jonathan Skinner wrote that he was reading Robert Creeley to girls pretty much from the get-go. So, on long night drives, my husband often recited "The Rain" to me, most winningly. Creeley's line break, which marked his rhythm, provoked sudden recognition. Except, being caught out, his line is inimitable. Readers can routinely recall their first hearing of a poem so marked. A poet from Missouri, when a nineteen-year-old soldier in Vietnam, described indolently fishing a Creeley title from the bottom of the mailroom's book box: *Binh Dinh province, 1968, discovering Creeley.* Thus another of us was born. "I Know a Man" is surely one of a handful of the most quoted and recited short poems of the twentieth century, along with Pound's "In a Station of the Metro," Williams's "The Red Wheelbarrow," Stevens's "Anecdote of the Jar," and Hughes's "Harlem." A current graduate student told me that when a high school teacher read "I Know a Man," it registered as one of those moments when she felt her hair being blown straight back behind her.

If one were to try to describe the heed
that poetry requires

Barbara Guest called it orchid attention. She felt the poem should tremble a little.
Fanny Howe affirmed a word had a vibratory presence. Genine Lentine wrote of
her process: "I let the leaves / come to the branch / and when the bee is at the /
blossom, I listen." About the occasional droughts she writes: "I spread my root hairs
and wait." I was reading a popular science book, titled *Every Living Thing*, focused
on pioneers in biology. The obsession that takes over these individuals is a thing to
ponder: the ones who consume uncountable hours of their lives on their tender
lab-mice-like bellies in the dirt of tropical forests watching army ants march over a
resting boa constrictor while the scientists try to pick out the beetles-disguised-as-
army-ants that follow and trick the ants into caring for them; the monomaniacal
types, e.g. Dan Janzen, whose project to name everything living in the Guanacaste
reserve in Costa Rica was forced to change venues years into the process, to the less
various Smokies, and when funding from magical Silicon pulled away from that
project, too, continued to press on with his All Taxa Biodiversity Inventory with one
intern—doomed without an army of ants and their guests to help, but oh so grand;
not to mention the decades spent trying to verify magnificent theories, often right
ones, such as Lynn Margulis's theory of endosymbiosis, accompanied by the
challenges of single-parenting, going without the encouragement of colleagues,
lacking the funds to support a lonely hypothesis that occurred to her in the splendor
of her youth and would consume the whole of her life and embody the entirety of
life… It's a goddamned crying shame, and oh so achingly critical what the great
dreamers and observers are seeing; only they possess the passion and the patience to
spread their root hairs and wait. Poetry has to command the same quality of attention,
if in shorter bursts but over a lifetime of them, and expect less in return than the
poetry deserves. As with most scientific papers, silence may be all that is at the other

end. Maybe silence itself has value beyond being humbling. Maybe the record being made is its primary worth, and the rest of our temporal span is meant just for living and for the attention it commands.

Of Those Who Can Afford to Be Gentle

I asked him, the visiting Chinese poet, because his work was so separate, so
distinct from much of what I had been reading by poets coming from China, how
he came to cultivate this way of writing; then I had to ask him, the visitor, where
he was on the night of June 4, 1989 (knowing he was the right age, that he was
already becoming an influential young poet, so it seemed reasonable that he would
have been there), and he told me: he was at home. He told me that a poet from out
of town phoned, wanted to meet with him, and so they met. They smoked and
talked into the late hours, and he did not hear, until by way of a call the following
day, what had happened, and when he went down toward the great square it was
blocked off, the ancient east–west artery of the city blocked off by tanks, many
tanks across Chang'an Jie. But what the poet most needed to say did not so much
concern the extent of his involvement or his removal from the epicenter of events:
only that he was one of four close friends, four young poets. Rather, he was the
only real survivor of this quartet.

One was taken by ambulance to the hospital, from the square. He had become
comatose during the weeks he lay in the hunger strike with the students, and
was taken by ambulance to Tiantan Hospital, but did not survive; he would be
cremated along with the others who died in the protest. And another of the
foursome had lain down on the railroad tracks two months earlier, while the
tensions were coalescing. And the third friend fled into exile and went mad in
Paris (from Paris he went to Rome, where he wrote increasingly deranged
letters to which the visiting poet could no longer respond, no longer knowing
what to say to becalm his friend). He, the visiting poet, did not commit suicide
or die in the hospital or flee and lose everything (his mind most of all) — he
stayed in Beijing. He married an artist. Had a son. Taught at the Central
Academy of Fine Arts.

I sensed a reticence to talk about his involvement, or rather his lack of involvement. I sensed he had keenly personal reasons for staying away, which he did not feel the need to explain, reasons that could have had more to do with temperament than politics. He did not want, nor was it expected of him, to explain his distance from the critical site at the critical moment. The term *Tiananmen Square Massacre,* he told me, was not accurate. It should be Chang'an Jie Massacre. *Chang'an* meaning eternal peace, and *Jie* meaning street, the route to the square where the soldiers actually opened fire. It is the city's first and most important street, built by the Last Great Khan, Kublai, for his armies of horses. The West called it the Tiananmen Square Massacre, which the Chinese government denied, and in fact the soldiers did not kill people on the square. The soldiers killed people who were on the way to the square. The people call it June 4. The government calls it June 4 Event; and in 1989 they called it June 4 Counterrevolutionary Upheaval. He stayed home on that historic evening.

He was a young Chinese man. An intellectual. He was a poet. He lost his friends. Three poets. And then he stopped writing. He stopped for several years. Not because he could not write or did not know how to write. (He had been a working journalist. I ask you, have you ever met a journalist at a loss for words?) He had earlier launched unofficial magazines of poetry; he was already a known writer, but he did not want to proceed in the way he had been proceeding — trying to be a "good" poet — writing like his peers, writing like his heroes, writing like the modernists — writing like Yeats, for example, or Eliot or like the Misty Poets who were already writing the way they would continue to write — because even to be a young male, to be an intellectual, to edit unofficial journals, to be, then, an unofficial poet, was to be implicated, and it meant, on some level or other, to lose. He began to think he was a fool, a pretender, and now that his friends were gone, now that he alone remained, the rest did not matter. He did not choose to write about June 4 as a journalist or as a poet (though he would edit a thousand-page collection by one of the fallen poets). He needed, he said, "something as strong as, as heavy as, as dark, crazy, turbulent as, the year." 1989.

And though he had not written directly of the massacre, he did not want his name to appear, eighteen years later, not because his identity would be obvious (if any big official ears were interested) but because they were his dead friends. He did not want to *make use,* as he put it, of their deaths. But for several years he had just stopped altogether. The old way of writing "would not fulfill" his aim. He wanted to create his own small literary cosmos qualified to respond to the giant wave of history. He began to develop an idea of writing "at a point between two ends — between poetry and history, between poetry and philosophy, poetry and religion."

Of course, as we know, the student movement was quashed. The intellectuals, and the workers in the city who had not benefited from the glasnost in Russia as they had hoped, and the laborers who had not gained from the market reforms, and the officials who had sympathized with the protests — those who did not die, flee into exile, or go mad — were detained, curtailed, or purged. His own silence was self-imposed. He also said, the visiting poet, it wasn't until he was at a writers' conference in Copenhagen fifteen years later that someone asked what he called "a sudden question," which was: why had he stayed in China? It seemed quite natural to him, being Chinese, to remain in China. "I chose," he replied, "to stay with my fate." He had to find his language, he said, had to find "a symmetry between my writing and the Chinese society." This led first to not writing, and then to writing, as he called it, "zigzag."

In the years since the first significant challenge to the Chinese state in more than four decades, there have been far, far higher civilian body counts in other parts of the world (though in only a minority of instances as direct retaliation for peaceful demonstrations). The poets who became important symbols of the June 4 events are either those who were not in the country at the time, and could not return, or those who left the country, some at risk of arrest and some not. And inside, since Tiananmen, many began to enjoy, within limits, the autonomy of international urban life. The visiting writer, the poet who stayed with his fate, stayed silent, and began again, reconnecting with his language one word at a time — *bird, bicycle, city, fire, peony* — in a series of prose poems that commence with literal and naive elaborations on the simple nouns and turn toward skeptical, if not wryly antagonistic, investigations of naming and meaning-making. All this, to what end, what end. "Only when a nail pierced through my hand did my hand reveal the truth; only when black smoke choked me to tears could I feel my existence. Riding sidesaddle on a white horse ten fairies tore up my heart." Zigzag. Learn to love the enigma, learn to love the paradox. Speak again.

In a Word,
a World

I like nouns that go up: *loft.* And ones that sink: *mud.* I like the ones that peck: *chicken.* And canter: *canter.* Those that comfort: *flannel* and *pelt. Cell* is an excellent word, in that it sweetly fulfills its assigned sound in a small, thin container. Unlike *hell,* which is disappointing. Overall. Wanting in force and fury. I like that a lone syllable names a necessary thing: *bridge, house, door, food, bed.* And the ones that sustain us: *dirt, milk,* and so on. What a thing, that a syllable — *birth, time, space, death* — points to the major mysteries with such simplicity, as with a silent finger. And to our very vital parts: *head, snout, heart, butt.* And our fundamental feeling: *fear.*

Nuptials & Violence

Deborah's wedding dress was made by a former East German Olympic gymnast, Ute Porath, who sews for the film industry and is based in Vancouver and New Orleans. The silk dress, lined with drapery fabric, was worn inside out, stitched with transfers from Kevin's molecular research and billets-doux between the biologist and the photographer. The lacy shoes were handcrafted in Burbank and arrived the day before vows were exchanged. The groom wore his one-time jacket.

The attendants stood on the twin staircase of a wiped-out Katrina house and spun their big paper flowers during the reading of the epithalamion. Walker's pulled pork and a high-end champagne were served to everyone's capacity.

After the nuptials the Pine Leaf Boys of Lafayette performed for revelers who ground their dancing shoes in the asphalt, armpits going all goaty.

The mosquito-stuffed martins rested under the causeway, and the stinkdamp spread along the far side of the lake. The repulsive orange teeth of the nutria went to work on the roots of grasses in the canals. Heavily armed men began to troll the streets behind the tinted windows of SUVs. Blotter time. Three men down.

Sirens were heard now and then, but between Arts and Music only kissing occurred under a full, howling NOLA moon, clouds copulating with abandon.

The old business about form & content

I am not among the hardhats dismissive of identifiable content, on the contrary, but poetry that does not really take language seriously into account—make that foremost: its texture, smell, shape, strength, options, registers, tonalities, etymologies, as well as its wide margins of error; how loudly it can play, how softly, and so forth; poetry that does not take formal acts into account: those weird, elusive organizing openings that the material presents, whether form is an extension of content or content is an extension of form, without obtaining to some sense of form—I cannot distinguish it from prose to any credible degree necessitating it being "a poem." Do I contradict myself? Very well then I contradict myself. It's a poem if I say it is. In his notebooks Oppen declared in his declarative way, "Form is what makes the thing graspable so you can know what is being said and why it was said and how it weighs. Until it takes form you haven't written it."

In Another Book That Brenda Wrote
Practical Water

Empire, destruction, imagination & wilderness: Brenda Hillman's "Hydrology of California" doesn't attempt to reconcile one event or thing with another because she aims to take in the wild scramble for life on planet Earth even if she has to open a fire hydrant onto our duct-taped-gaping eyes and toothpick-propped-wide mouths while she empties her recitation of waterways and their fate. The abecedary backs up the poem, but remains incidental. Suppose there is a point from which you cannot be held back. Therein lies your unimproved poem of perfection; "no one knows how this sentence will end in a dream with a lyric sky."

Of Those Who Can Afford to Be Gentle
I'll say it again

Poetry, I have tardily determined, not only seeks silence, it aspires to silence. I mean not that it aims for perfection but for an opening, an unofficial opening, a zone wherein the language affords unexpected associations and alternative outcomes. For poet George Oppen the egregious breach between word and world resulted in a silence (again, self-imposed) of twenty-five years. "Only one thing remained reachable," wrote Paul Celan, after Auschwitz, "close and secure amid all losses: language.... But it had to go through its own lack of answers, through terrifying silence, through the thousand darknesses of murderous speech." Perhaps he asked too much of words: to go through, to come through. They could not protect him from murdering himself despite a radical effort on his part to remake or destroy the German language in order to save it. It is not that writing poetry from the nearness of a massacre or in the tumult of social transformation is not doable, but that writing poetry is a highly inflected and reflective activity. Poets may react to events as they unfold, but poetry exacts its own time and toll and turn. Or so I have mostly been conditioned to think and am not for the first time calling into question. It is not that writing poetry in the wake of one historical nightmare after another is obscene, as Adorno famously and hopelessly declared post-Holocaust, or even that *not to write* poetry may be the real obscenity as Adorno later recanted—but first, silence. And then, zigzag: *bird, bicycle, peony.* William Vollmann concluded a seven-volume treatise on violence in less time than most poets can produce one obdurate poem on the blood we keep shedding. "The isolated man is dead, his world around him exhausted // And he fails! He fails, that meditative man!" wrote George Oppen; yet a few passages later, in five lines he distilled man's overproved habit of war: "It is the air of atrocity, / An event as ordinary / As a President. // A plume of smoke, visible at a distance / In which people burn"—lines much in keeping with the thirteenth-century Mongol aria from which these lines, alas, cover the ages: Empires rise / People suffer / / Empires fall / People suffer.

I may have to allow that poetry's overproved slowness is part of the reason it, too, is becoming a casualty. It is not merely that images have displaced its authority, but speed has set aside its function of relaying information. I would have to qualify this allowance with the tenacious feeling that our enduring function as seers is not only intact but is also being pressed back into urgent service. Obviously some of us see better and farther than others, and by *seeing* I mean nothing so hieratic as prophecy but something more workaday, such as rectifying the word. Trueing what is seen. The *n*th of acuity is not a given of the art but a time-honored goal.

Poetry's long-lived epics are rife with the terrible acts of gods and of men such as Gilgamesh (those poor cedar trees); the protracted clashes of the Kyrgyz for independence in the Manas epic; the prolific hecatombs in "the poem of force," as Simone Weil tagged *The Iliad*, and in the *Mahabharata*, what someone else tagged "*The Iliad* on acid". Rivers of gore run through the poetic record.

"Opening the book of what happened" is but one defining motivation behind poetry now. I think of Carolyn Forché's "On Earth" and Edward Kleinschmidt's lesser-known "To Remain." Even in elegy, poetry persists not just to remember but also to ratify our existence. "That we too passed," Hardy wrote of our passage, thus engraving our presence. Even in the corners of the world, poetry aims for the long view. Allen Grossman says its function is human discourse, its function is "the keeping of the image of persons as precious in the world." Poetry pertains to universal solidarity. A tent set up in Baghdad for poets to read in — Sunni on one side, Shiite on the other. Separate but together. There to listen. To one another. There for. Each other. Human discourse. Breaking silence. Staying violence.

The entire lower lip would lift upwards then sink back to its original
place. She would then gather both lips and protrude them in a pout taking
in the breath that might utter some thing. (One thing. Just one.)
                                         Theresa Hak Kyung Cha

At least among American poets, the documentary vision intertwined with the
lyric impulse has asserted itself with sporadic intensity, usually responsive to
events and conflicts of historic proportion—the Depression, the struggle for civil
rights, war, always war. I am readily reminded of Charles Reznikoff's *Testimony*,
composed from pouring through state court records beginning in 1885; and
Muriel Rukeyser's "Book of the Dead," confronting a cover-up of silica-mining
conditions in West Virginia: "What three things can never be done," she asks.
"Forget. Keep silent. Stand alone," she answers. I think also of Frank Stanford's
picaresque tear across the racial divide in *The Battlefield Where the Moon Says I
Love You*. Of Martha Collins's *Blue Front*, a book-length lyric of a lynching in
Cairo, Illinois, potentially witnessed by her father when he was five. Of "What I
Heard About Iraq," by Eliot Weinberger, largely drawn from another poet's
hoard from the world press:

> I heard Colonel Nathan Sassaman say: "With a heavy dose of fear and
> violence, and a lot of money for projects, I think we can convince these
> people that we are here to help them."

> I heard Richard Perle say: "Next year at about this time, I expect
> there will be a really thriving trade in the region, and we will see rapid
> economic development. And a year from now, I'll be very surprised if
> there is not some grand square in Baghdad named after President Bush."

Examples that show that even transcription can attain to what Maurice Blanchot calls "that big word," *transcendence.*

The lyric mode dominant, Forrest Gander's "Burning Towers, Standing Wall" is a serial meditation in which everything about a Mayan wall, at once evanescent and terrible — the "pair of trogons [that] sit like lords on the ruin / where rocks flake away in rain and birdshit"; the shadows of boys who have run in the wall's shadow, its particular scent and sounds "nearly the same sounds *they* heard"; and the "spikes of vengeance" and blood that its centuries have absorbed — is meticulously recorded and imagined.

Among the titles on my book-cluttered desk are *All Day Permanent Red,* one of Christopher Logue's loose-lipped takes on *The Iliad,* and Danish writer Inger Christensen's *alphabet,* which limpidly, formally lays its readers open to the capacity and penchant of our species for total annihilation. Between the first word and the last, however, many rude utterances need to be expended to interrupt the silence, most of them brought into effect by the actual violence in which they are bounded. And I have just elected for the occasion to discuss, in brief, collective violence — I could have addressed the violence of the white page, the violence of line breaks, beauty's celebrated convulsiveness or its caustic end.

Cha again:

> It murmurs inside. It murmurs. Inside is the pain of speech the pain to say. Larger still. Greater than is the pain not to say. To not say. Says nothing against the pain to speak. It festers inside. The wound, liquid, dust. Must break. Must void.

In a time in which my own country has embarked on war without end, without borders or accountability, practicing what the CIA terms *extraordinary rendition* and journalist Jane Mayer calls *outsourcing torture*—her assertion chronicles beatings, whippings, burnings; prisoners being urinated upon, having electrical wires attached to their genitals; water-boarding, forced suppositories—it is hard to imagine poetry obtaining its essential silence, though its overall movement is to establish a clearing. Poetry may proceed zigzag (see Xi Chuan). It may take the words out of their lying teeth (see Weinberger). It may make a monument of the alphabet (see Christensen) or a memorial of rosebushes planted at the cardinal points (see Kleinschmidt). It may stare long and hard at a very old wall (see Gander). Whenever poets seek to penetrate the "insanity in high places" (see Oppen), poetry has to counter its inherent diffidence, its isolationist tendencies. To speak. Again.

My examples are happenstance, and there are countless others. They are among those in which the poets found, borrowed, revived, or invented means that they could apply to their medium and bind to the "collective undercurrent" wherein the subject becomes more than an object. It is only at this point that Adorno could still endorse a poetry that "actually bears the whole in mind and is not simply an expression of the privilege, refinement, and gentility of those who can afford to be gentle."

Poets will have to summon a fierceness equal to the current environment. We will have to meet irrational force with savage insight. We will have to bring our own rudimentary technology, our own order, to the common weal. Inasmuch as poetry is the mind's domain, it is the mind's defense. But poets will have to shed some of our mental armor. We will have to channel our loathing toward our elected objects of negation, forego gentle murmurings (as Adorno says, "There is nothing innocuous left"). Poets will have to stop bemoaning poetry's lost station, while continuing to press its perceptions. That which we cannot speak of we can no longer pass over in silence. Mostly, poets will fail. The structures will fail. Words will fumble and fall. But in so failing and fumbling poets refuse to be accomplices. We continue to articulate the possibility of solidarity. Human discourse. Continuity. At the onset of his *History of the Conquest of Mexico,* William Prescott wrote of Montezuma's nonresistance to evil. No more of that. There are haunting, indelible marks to be made before our abandonment of words can be complete. Poets in our day will have to draw down against our latent subversiveness and punch through the dream hole to that opening wherein listening is possible and violence is not inevitable.

From the back of her neck she releases her shoulders free. She swallows once more. (Once more. One more time would do.) In preparation. It augments. To such a pitch. Endless drone, refueling itself. Autonomous. Self-generating. Swallows with last efforts last wills against the pain that wishes it to speak. (See Cha.)

*(Went to hear a young man talk about what could be a one-book affair with writing;
then I read Ishmael Beah's traumatic account of being a child soldier in Sierra Leone.
Watching a* Rambo *sequel, the boys stopped the movie to go wipe out a village, and
returned to watch the rest as if from intermission; then went out again through the forest
to murder more people. One stunning day they came upon a village unexpectedly, a
younger boy asked Beah — a child himself — to hold off the group in his charge
because the younger boy wanted to try out some of his Rambo moves before the others
began attacking. A child, armed with an AK-47, cranked up on cocaine cut with
gunpowder and* Rambo.*

*Whether or not the incessant onslaught of senseless images plays a part in senseless
slaughter, my thinking is that poetry has a part to play in repulsing the same. The flame
of continuity, human discourse, flickers in its structures. Inasmuch as it is a modulated and
thoughtful engagement, it is to some degree an enterprise at odds with itself.)*

Spring & All

1923: Wallace Stevens's *Harmonium* was published, Mina Loy's *Lunar Baedecker*, Jean Toomer's unassimilable hybrid masterwork, *Cane*, and *Spring and All*, an equally unassimilable hybrid masterwork. That year, Yeats, whose dominance in poetry was commonly acknowledged, was awarded the Nobel Prize. Marianne Moore's *Observations* and Gertrude Stein's *The Making of Americans* were soon to clear the horizon. The former would be as steady on its feet as a wading bird; the latter, a bollard of granite. The leonine-haired Ezra Pound was the force upon which many depended and with which all had to contend. Staying on his own side of the Atlantic afforded William Carlos Williams the breathing room he needed.

The Book That Brenda Wrote
Seasonal Works with Letters On Fire

This is mini-BH's conversation with mega-BH:

An attempted dialogue with the darkest forces

Arguments ensuing

She doesn't lose her head

This is her open letter to the world

There is always time out for a baby, always

time to think of a friend's loss, time for a domestic frenzy

with the gentle mother, time for a little silly

singing down dilly down and the communal mysteries of ritual

as "a snake slithers over serpentine / then down to the first

dark where every cry has size —"

A fascination with things the more minute they come

A fascination with the galaxies

A fascination with things more illusory than can be proved

A fascination with letters, with vowels, with typographic marks,

fonts, captions, illustration, the Latin names of plants,

the onomatopoeia of birdsong, chatter in the understory

Little BH is not a drone

Big BH neither

She would not have us unloose the drone

She would have us "keep roundness"

"everything / means everything plus / there is no hidden meaning —"

So much color, so much motion, so many "xeroxed copies

of the dream," "a georgics of cleaning," everything, you dig

while the universe is speeding up and letters on fire

from one who "never / doubted poetry — anxiously

taking vermillion tones past / disappointed citizenship—"
Words push through the entropy of self-involvement
Her iambic rejoinder to whoever would "tweet & sleep
through the wars":

"We hope to learn to breathe before we die."

Hold Still, Lion

The Creeley line inevitably alerts and pleasures our motor impulses. Creeley attributed the delay in his line to Charlie Parker. He also credited the musician for his active treatment of the silences. I liken the poet's jarring line to stepping off an unseen curb and righting oneself midair. The recovery delivers a quick exhilaration.

+ + +

Creeley prose: the syntax had the formal air of a previous era, yet it held to the same hard definition: nothing superfluous. The complex he called poems simply made their moves faster. The writing stayed with the experience, stayed with the making. Autobiographical, of course, but in the sense that "writing could be an intensely specific revelation of one's own content." The seriousness of his project keeps to a continuum. He lived, he lives, his life in words, "bringing all the world to one instant of otherwise meaningless 'time.'"

Jean Valentine, Abridged

Valentine's palette is mostly grey. Next comes blue (borage, cobalt, silk, robe, egg). Then white. Some inherent greens. But she draws most often from the greyer end of the grey scale. It could be manifest in a postmortem jaw, dusty glass, a sky, one degree Fahrenheit, a lone sock under a sickbed; the water is grey, and the long wall where one exits a car. Grey is the intermediate state she inhabits with no apparent effort. In the grey space, the bardo, the spirit starts to find shape, to find internal structure.

Spring & All

Yet, for the mash-up of affinities, free-floating associations, and spasms of anger, Williams loved simplicity and order. He avoided the sesquipedalian habits of Pound and Eliot. The stripped-down poems in *Spring and All* are as quick and unencumbered as any nude tripping down the stairs. The choice enjambment ("under the surge of the blue / mottled clouds"), the lucent precision of the modest noun *glaze*, and the assertion that "the rose is obsolete" were stock-in-trade. He delivered the language scrubbed clean, made new.

+ + +

This was a gutsy, self-conscious generation of writers and artists. They all knew each other. Pound and H.D. and the painter, Charles Demuth, to whom *Spring and All* is dedicated, were friends from the college years. Williams was soon to befriend Wallace Stevens and Marianne Moore and Mina Loy. The Stieglitz crowd. Duchamp and the collector Walter Arensberg, and on and on. They promoted and financed one another's dreams, shared and competed for lovers, for recognition and influence. Williams's profession planted him. In the city, the painters seeded his ideas. While his inaugural reading of "Overture to a Dance of Locomotives" was impressive, it was not enough to persuade Ms. Loy to lie with him.

Jean Valentine, Abridged

She has laid in her own basic set of signs: breath, milk, water, hand, bone, bowl, grass, door, room, bed, and boat. Her chalupa, her painted, flat-bottomed boat, rowboat, raft, dory, nightboat; the cold house itself is "a turned-over boat." Who rows and under whose power? Even the wings of the wild geese she summons from a former husband's dream are "rowing, laborious, wood against wood." Where going? Happiness, I suppose; toward happiness. Agnes Martin writes that happiness is the very thing we want to serve. Happiness is what we were born to serve. The way there is far. Too far. What, then, can we obtain in its stead? *Gratitude,* like the paintings by Agnes. Which is near. But at what point does the journey end? "Before the ramp Contentment." And that is where Jean Valentine was compelled to write that she came up short, "stopped like a horse." Anne, Agnes, Jean: theirs is not a system of theories, not a representation of portents, but a commitment to the labor. "Writing a word // changing it."

The Orchidaceous Ms. Loy,
the Amaranth, the Octopus

In her midthirties Mina Loy to New York City from Paris. She had long before dropped out of art school. Traveled. Married badly. Had affairs. Divorced. Lost a child. Left her two surviving children in someone else's care for a time. She had already been exposed to all the currents of the art world, and seemed to have some facility for everything that caught her attention. Her love poems ("Songs to Joannes") are described by her biographer Carolyn Burke as "a peculiar kind of war poetry," though critics tend to focus on the body as the centerfold of this sequence, an audacious send-up of the romantic love poem. Bear in mind, this is writing that finds words delicious and will not have them chained to the wall of denotation. Being bourgeois was not her line of work. Her famous poem "Lunar Baedeker" is, for the traveling reader, a near-hallucinatory trip: "Delirious Avenues / lit / with the chandelier souls / of infusoria / from Pharaoh's tombstones" lead not to your next Best Western.

+ + +

H.D.'s "Fragment Forty-One," in her book *Heliodora,* casts the emblems of love in a whole new salt-encrusted light, priming a writing career that would take on the male preserve of the epic and refigure Greek mythos from the female's ground:

> I was not blind when I turned.
> I was not indifferent when I strayed aside
> or loitered as we three went
> or seemed to turn a moment from the path
> for that same amaranth.

I was not dull and dead when I fell
back on our couch at night.
I was not indifferent when I turned
and lay quiet.
I was not dead in my sleep.

No, H.D. was not blind. She contained multitudes and made radical choices for her era, including the perspective of the literary and idealized figure of the female as the author of her own life. The adrenaline rushes and risks of war and love stamped her early work. She and her long-term partner Bryher (née Annie Winifred Ellerman) were among the holdouts during the Blitz of London. The first section of H.D.'s *Trilogy*, "The Walls Do Not Fall," rolls out sequences of short couplets in which she makes her stand for the endurance of love, selfhood, and poetry—against the odds, beseeching "Isis, the great enchantress, / in her attribute of Serqet, // the original great-mother, / who drove // harnessed scorpions / before her." There is both a layering of symbols and upending of their significance, a cutting to the cryptic bone, and a trove of autobiographical hints behind the persona "H.D.":

be firm in your own small, static, limited

orbit and the shark-jaws
of outer circumstance

will spit you forth:
be indigestible, hard, ungiving,

so that, living within,
you beget, self-out-of-self,

and would proclaim poetry the redemptive successor to violence:

O Sword,

you are the younger brother, the latter-born,

your Triumph, however exultant,
must one day be over,

in the beginning
was the Word.

Though H.D. did not stay at Bryn Mawr, she was there long enough to get wrapped up with Pound for a time, long enough to meet Marianne Moore (and would in fact publish Moore's poems in the *Egoist* when she was the editor).

+ + +

Marianne Moore ended up in New York. After college she taught at a Native American school in Pennsylvania. She even taught the great footballer Jim Thorpe. In New York, she worked as a part-time librarian. There's something peculiarly fitting about her as a New York poet. She was both an anachronism and a modernist. Her use of syllabics was true to her sound and sense, and while syllabics were experimented with by other modernists, none were as committed as Moore: even she was occasionally willing to break step with her count. Quotation and collage were a standard part of her toolbox. They are rife in the well-known poems "Marriage" and "An Octopus." She had a most particularizing sense of description, setting one thing utterly apart from anything else on Earth or comparing one thing to an utterly dissimilar other. More than anyone of her time, Ms. Moore deployed the most unexpected, underused word. "Ecstasy affords / the occasion and expediency determines the form." There is no one else like her.

If the nineteenth-century novel cannot be bested, if the sonnet has to perform recombinative hijinks to hang on to its nomenclature, if the essay has to outmaneuver the theorists to lay claim to its inventive literariness/and so forth, then it is no shocker that growing numbers of writers are gamboling into other media and other genres to slip away from their own hardpan enclosures—if only to return as fouled and bedraggled rejects, grateful to have a pen to call home. A genre then is a place to get away from and a place to come back to. A shelter for the wayward among us.

Accessing photos, newspaper columns, letters; improvising a road trip, interviews, questionnaires; pilfering board games, inventing inventories, visiting outsider artists, specialists, and archives—all this requires constantly moving the corners when not removing them altogether. The old term belles lettres *has fallen off, but in English Beautiful Letters could be construed expansively until you have something booksome. Meanwhile I opt for* Words by . . .

THE POEM

A poetry of the meaning of words
And a bond with the universe

I think there is no light in the world
but the world

And I think there is light

Oppen

If a lifetime were spent trying to determine why one did what one did — e.g.,
gather leeches, terminate wayward cells, defy gravity, or commit a succession of
white-collar crimes without compunction or consequences, or any number of
preferences one might be born lucky enough to exercise or come under the
protection of — one would have a hard time coming up with a better reason than:
meaning, bond, world, light. Who wouldn't want to be a member of that club.
Who could have achieved a better expression and distillation thereof. To suggest a
purpose to being here for which humans are amazingly and imaginatively
equipped, and then to follow through as if it were true, because one believed it
true, and then along came the opening and the will with a very small sack of
words by which to nail that goal to the page...

Michael Ondaatje's

DRIVING WITH DOMINIC
IN THE SOUTHERN PROVINCE
WE SEE HINTS OF THE CIRCUS

The tattered Hungarian tent

A man washing a trumpet
at a roadside tap

Children in the trees,

one falling
into the grip of another

Think of it as a spell, a moment broken off from all the moments that surround it, touched with the mystery of being which Ondaatje's writing honors with such scrupulous consistency. That for me is the pith of the poem's appeal. It is not a poem that requires an exegesis. It is meant to be transparent. Not set with astounding technical precision, but kept purposely plain. I have long linked two sentences from Eudora Welty's *The Optimist's Daughter* to the effect Ondaatje's writing has on a reader: "The boat came breasting out of the mist, and in they stepped. All new things in life were meant to come like that." This is what his quick, understated poem delivers.

A poem of six short lines with a title of three short lines, half the length of the poem's body. At the very least, with the long title the physical scene is apt to be presented, as it is here. This makes building a set inside the body unnecessary. We are located. Too often a poem's basic content is rendered in the title. A regrettable act, title plunked down as village explainer. The touch in this instance is more deft and discreet: the speaker is in the car and can be presumed to be the passenger. The driver is a man named Dominic. Only his first name is given, which implies familiarity: friendship, kinship, or the first-name basis of a tour guide's tag (proper name afforded to the customer).

The passenger is free to look out the side window as well as the windshield. First sighting is assigned to the passenger. They are driving in the Southern Province. In this instance we can guess with little risk that the speaker-passenger is the poet, a famed writer, conditioned not to miss anything, especially something magical. The undeveloped Southern Province of Sri Lanka is the author's native country (an area not then severely damaged by the tsunami), a place he left in childhood, so his interest in what he sees is intensified by every return. Every return offers an opportunity to fill in the gaps, further detailing the imagination with what his senses actually testify to. His senses are inundated. Sri Lanka.

Their mutual silence is implied. The shell of the car separates them from what is exterior. A private space is established. The space elides with time: here, now gone. Both have been privileged to take in the scene — which creates its own bond. They can confirm each other's chance vision. They shared this.

The reader flashes on *La Strada:*
a slice of film history appears on the mind's screen and runs full length, the reel
breaking here and there to stand in for lapses of memory, for forward motion of the
car, for changes of scene. The passenger's relation to film is well documented. There
is no persona to construct the poem; the passenger melts into the scenery. He is the
camera and does not break the frame after the title announces his presence.

The poem itself is a trace of that
title. It is the trace that attracts most of all. The poem describes a sighting, a
glimpse of another world, other lives, the kind of thing one feels so charmed to
have witnessed, to which one's own life is wistfully kindred but definitively
removed. Vivified in an instant — with a couple of bare details — a corner of the
world where circus people still provide entertainment, live a nomadic existence,
get drinking and cleaning water from a spigot sticking out of the ground. A
suspended state of childhood where children do what children have always done:
climb trees. However, these children are professionals. They are trapeze artists,
and the tree provides a natural armature for an informal rehearsal. As children,
they can fall and trust their bodies. As professionals they can fall, trust one to
catch the other. The grip is abrupt; it holds. The poem is barely there before the
scene peels away behind the driver and his passenger, but the trace lingers, and
that is just very, very pleasing... releasing our own hushed reverie.

There are no grand strategies at
work in this poem. There is no sabotage to syntax or sequence. There is no
pronounced rhythm. No ulterior philosophical message. With terrific economy a
lush environment is suggested. With characteristic restraint a little world is made.
One blogger dismissed the poem as something written as easily as striking a match
and blowing it out. It could well have been so simply bestowed, that effortlessly
executed. The poem could be the nucleus of one of the central characters and
narratives of a novel to come. *Divisadero,* for instance. I suggest that it is.

Jean Valentine, Abridged

She never forgets her friends, her family, her exes. She cannot. "How in dreams you are everyone: / awake too you are everyone." She takes her place in the full measure and motion of the procession. She is at the bedside or grave of her parents, her friends. Holds the hand of fever. When the time comes she is vacuuming up the sock of her dying friend. When the time comes she is the muse of palliative care. The setting is Intensive Care.

+ + +

These are poems only a woman could write. Poems that could issue only from the womb of woman-mind. They constitute a visible, visceral response to an inward, spiritual struggle. The struggle is mighty. The struggle is in the living, and the worth of it is never doubted. "Equally at home," Anne Truitt writes after a great storm, "with both violence and tranquility. How they complement and validate one another."

+ + +

City artists, city writers but not composing in a city register. They are not manic. The work does not seek society. Not especially active in the life of the street. They are in season. They are headed straight for the center of some unnameable flower.

Anne Truitt's sentinels, standing straight, illimitable. Resistant to gravity.

Agnes Martin's canvases gessoed by her aged hand with broad slaps of the brush. Preparing herself to make something beautiful. "Beauty is the mystery of life. It is not in the eye it is in the mind." And from Martin's *Writings:* "In our minds, there is awareness of perfection."

+ + +

A poet who brandishes her strange and irreducible lines like an antenna broken off of a radio, like a caduceus.

According to Pound, William Carlos Williams was the "hardiest specimen in these parts." While zealously promoting the supremacy of the imagination, Williams dealt in real things, with individuals in real and current need. In his line of work, people were literally exposed. Then there was the endless variety of the species, which suited what he referred to as his nervous nature. Then everything along the roadside just popped out and demanded his immediate attention. He was a local. He was "seeking to articulate," seeking "to name it." He resisted revision. He loved art. He spoke "plain American." He had a thirst for *now*. And he had his own beat, "a certain unquenchable exaltation," as he said of his renowned wheelbarrow. The excitement the writing exuded is as *contagious* today as when he made his rounds "quickened with life about him." The reader is induced to stay awake. Make contact. Look ahead. In 1923, poetry's backward advance came to the crossroads. The pediatrician from Rutherford discharged the symbolic heap of myth and metaphor; adjusted his focal length to light up cast-off, common things; dug his heels into American dirt and passed directly into the moment. Ah, SPRING.

Hold Still, Lion

The reading Creeley was to give the spring of 2005 for Harvard's Phi Beta Kappa Literary Exercises would go on. The prize he was to be given in June in Modena, Italy, was awarded. Death notwithstanding. Robert Creeley Day at Acton, Massachusetts, takes place again this year, drizzle or downpour. The memorials began almost immediately on a host of websites and blogs; eulogies and elegies were posted to the ends of the literate world, which is the end of *a* world. *So there.* With the deaths of original mentors and so many of his dearest peers, he felt "the company," as he called the body politic of poetry, getting smaller. "Now no one seems there anymore." And taking his note, today one counts not the mighty voices of the 1950s now silenced, but the smaller number yet singing. Conversely, in the instance of Robert Creeley, the company was still growing. We are also his company, and his persistent voice made us and has kept us so. Embarrassed, as many are, by the designation *poet,* he became one "by virtue of the act of writing." And for him, it became not only "a place to be" or "a consistently present reality" but *the* place, *the* reality. He did not play at being a poet — though pleasure was central to his preoccupation; he worked at it, locating himself altogether in words. He was a man of his words. He was *given* to write poems.

Jean Valentine, Abridged

"Happiness.   Beauty.   Art.
— That bird seems to like you.
— Yes, that bird knows
there's not much time."

She is a dream barker.

She is a messenger.

She flies. With one wing.

She wraps her long arms
around a globe of light.

She stands outside the light.

She is a ghost star of the past. The
guest in the ghost car.

She hovers.

She leaves Ireland. She had to leave.

She is running for a train / an older woman on her back.

She is an inmate. A patient. A healer.

She followed the string in the dark.

She is alone. She is alone.

She wrote a book.

Her hands and face and ears are covered with bees.

She carried a dead deer.

She is at the door.

Door in the mountain / let her in. Love let her in. Her name is "She Sang."

The son was in high school. He had a part-time job
at a laundromat in a small disenchanting strip mall.
He was reading *Anna Karenina*. He was three hundred–
plus pages deep. Soap 'n' Suds was almost never busy.
The boss was scarce. The son could read. A young woman
arrived with her wash, got change, and asked what he
was reading. *Anna Karenina*. Oh, she said, is that the
one where she throws herself on the rails at the end.

Asshole, he muttered.

¿LE GUSTA ESTE JARDÍN

QUE ES SUYO?

¡EVITE QUE SUS HIJOS LO DESTRUYAN!

It was so long ago but this novel holds up as one of those transfixing reads—
snatch this book out of my hands at your own risk. I was traveling through the
Yucatán on second-class buses with my college roommate Shelby. There was
everything to be seen out the window, especially as my foreign travel had been so
meager and actual encounters with dramatically different landscapes so limited,
but I could only look up and out when the reading and the ride began to jiggle my
vision and roil my intestines. We had left the Ozarks, left Fayetteville, where the
University of Arkansas is situated and where Shelby and I shared a small duplex,
for a summer in New Orleans. But when we got to New Orleans we could not find

an apartment; we did not begin to know where to look for a job. The heat hammered us though we had each bought a spaghetti-strap sundress in Memphis. We were hanging out at a friend's double-shotgun rental. Drinking beer, smoking cigarettes, reading poetry. Talking a more or less impotent advocacy of radicalism. We were only fluent in drinking and smoking. Someone there was wearing a bill cap with GARP printed on it, the first extraneous product I had encountered to promote a book. Someone else mentioned he was going to the Yucatán the next morning. His name was Joe, and I seem to remember he wound up becoming a prominent tenor in Paris. In an understated pitch delivered in dulcet tones, he made the Mexican peninsula sound paradisiacal. A couple of days later my friend and I were headed for the Yucatán, too. We couldn't have had $400 between us, including airfare. Mérida was just as withering as New Orleans, but everything was in a different language. The bus ride from the airport to the centro was an eyeful. Poincianas and jacarandas, frangipani and yellow oleander. Houses with unfinished second floors jutting rebar in every direction. A hen pecking at my bag while I clung to the overhead bar, a suckling baby swathed in the mother's rebozo. Ribby meat dangling from hooks in open-air stands, retread tire shops, panaderías in the path of clouds of engine exhaust, kids kicking a soccer ball in the dust. Mérida was a low-storied town, earthquake country. A dense grid of look-alike buildings that made it difficult to orient yourself except by the zocalo. There were interior gardens and birds in aviaries, fresh-squeezed juices, iguanas on rope leashes, handmade cotton hammocks, ceiling fans and louvered windows; extravagant courtesies and saturated colors to which I was unaccustomed, noises that seemed festive even when they were just bleating car horns. Mérida was a base, but when you set out to travel, a night barely passes before the urge to see what's in the next pueblo propels the morning.

A pair of jeans, a sundress, a couple of tees, and nylon tube backpacks. I was armed with the necessary book. I don't remember who first put the book on my list or how it came into my possession, but when I pulled it out of my pack on the first leg of the journey Shelby groaned, having left her own in NOLA. She'd broken with the first absolute of travel: you have to bring your own read. Never mind that I owed her. For starters my pissy blue-point Siamese had run off her handsome, peace-loving six-toed cat; yet I coldly obstructed her reading over my shoulder, and was easily triggered if she made the teensiest effort to ease mi libro over to her seat at the first sign of a light siesta. But by the time we had swerved, grounded, screeched, and convulsed our way through the mountains to San Cristóbal de las Casas, Shelby was visibly sick. Her underwear had to be disposed of in the bus stop at Villahermosa. When we rumbled into the old Mayan city in the valley of the highlands, we found a grungy place that grudgingly tolerated unchaperoned gringas and young stoner vagabonds. A dull bulb hung from a sketchy cord over our thinly blanketed cots. The great amenity was a common stucco steam room, the only place to get warm that didn't involve a vertical trek to a cantina. Shelby had the shivers and sweats really bad and I finally showed her a morsel of mercy. I tore the book apart up to the dog-eared page of my reading. She was grateful, though what she really needed was a doctor. We walked into the first of the lit doorways marked by a hand-done sign of a giant syringe. One good jab and a swab of alcohol and we were back on the cobbled alleyway. There was always a good sopa de pollo y ajo to be found. Always a bracing shot of cheap tequila. And now she had her share of a book. She was no mewler.

In those days I dreaded coming to the end of a mighty book. It was not so much the story; I just resisted being ejected from the experience. Furthermore, endings usually convinced me the whole apparatus was a setup. Later, I would come to read the last pages first to get that done with because I could not stand the tension, even if I had a canny inkling as to where the tale was going. But I finally came to the end of my Mexican travel book, passed the remainder over to Shelby, and she polished it off. Then we could relive it. The first thing she said was something about Yvonne being trampled by the dead indio's horse. *#%¡What are you talking about*#%! ¿How could I have missed that? Two-and-a-half pages of menacing prose committed to Yvonne's demise. I was furious. I must have looked up to gaze on the clouds rising below us, and the campesino tending his maíz on a precipice. My friend had to locate the passage for me to confirm. It's true, obvious even, the Consul's end you could smell coming long before he staggered into El Farolito. He was beyond saving himself, but when it came to pass, his dingy death, it couldn't have reached higher heights or more fathomless depths of prose than when he felt "his life slivering out of him like liver, ebbing into the tenderness of the grass. He was alone. Where was everybody? Or had there been no one. Then a face shone out of the gloom, a mask of compassion. It was the old fiddler, stooping over him. 'Compañero—' he began. Then he had vanished." Which is just a scintilla of the rapture, the "complete glutted oblivion," and the lonely degradation the novelist works into the terminal pages of el último réquiem for "those who have nobody with." It was a long, long mescal-fueled descent, the Day of the Dead in *Under the Volcano,* in the ominous shadow of El Popo "plumed with emerald snow and drenched with brilliance," before a dead dog is thrown down the ravine after our "great and shattered" hero.

Do you like this garden
that is yours?
See to it that your children do not
destroy it!

Then there is *Absalom, Absalom!*
But if I had told you that one, I'd be
a real asshole.

In a Word,
a World

The mother word, word of words, must pull everything in range to its skin if not its core. It must set one's head awhirling. It must whelm the mouth when spoken, and clobber the senses when confronted. It must include everyone everywhere. Forever. And so, *world*, Middle English, from the Old English *weorold*, also appearing as *warld, wardle, werld, worlde, worold, woruld, wurld, wuruld*—that's the word for me. Such surround-sound amplitude, such magnetic force. It cannot be got outside of. One must hew to its basic requirements or succumb to its anguish. "World. World. O world!" Made of everything and nothing.

(Poet Gale Nelson told me his all-time favorite blurb was one by Clark Coolidge of Michael Gizzi's Continental Harmony: *Reading this book cuts me a new stump.*

I think that should clear-cut the forest of blurbs.)

Questionnaire in January

Colette said writing leads only to writing. Where does it lead you. And what led you here.

To what mark are you attempting to hold yourself.

What do poets talk about. What do they have to talk about.

Into what forms do you see poetry pouring, morphing, shuddering.

Is there anything you see that poetry has the capacity to alter or altogether upend.

Agnes Martin said, of painting *White Flower,* she was trying to express the emotions we feel when we see grey geese descending.

Can you put words to an inchoate desire.

René Char writes, What can we do to bring the ship nearer to its longing.

Margaret Avison says poetry results when every word is written in the full light of all a writer knows.

Also Hirshfield

Can you fix anything. Anything at all.

Could a score be organized around your writing. Can you describe its shape. Can you describe its sound.

Does a voice apply to your thoughts distinct from talking.

In your memory, with what smell do you associate most powerfully. Evan Lavender-Smith writes, There are certain smells that have the power to dissolve the problem of life.... Sophia's head sweat.

If your goal was to forget yourself in your writing, what would you foreground in your stead.

James Hillman said, Get out of history, get into geography. What do you say.

Are you possessed by a topophilia. (The feeling of affection that individuals have for particular places, a term introduced by W.H. Auden, 1947. Places in this sense may vary in scale from a single room to a nation or continent. Topophilia is an important aspect of the symbolic meaning and significance of landscapes.)

Is the goal of community attainable through the gates of poetry.

Marianne Moore wrote of poetry: I, too, dislike it. Reading it, however, with a perfect contempt for it, one discovers in it, after all, a place for the genuine. What do you say.

Frank O'Hara said poetry is as useful as a machine. How so.

Beckett said the form must let the mess in.

Can you say something about the architecture of a poem.

About the visual plane.

What if a line were just something to which you arbitrarily added a virgule.

What is your area of "research."

What is your favorite body of water and why.

Identify a pattern in something other than a poem which you might apply to a poem. It could be an evacuation route, a small-town phone book, a crazy quilt, a roulette wheel, a menu, a ship's manifest, etc., etc.

Try composing a rhapsody on a single word.

Have you any tenets.

What is missing from your writing now.

How softly can you play.

Do you have an identifiable palette. (If you don't know what color to take, take black. Picasso).

Picasso said to always work against, even against oneself, and Morton Feldman said he worked by negation.

Your thoughts on the "career" of poetry.

In what regard to your life do you hold your poetry.

Genine Lentine writes of her process:

> I let the leaves
> come to the branch
> and when the bee is at the
> blossom, I listen.

And about drought:

> I spread my root hairs and wait.

What is your physical experience of poetry.

What commands your attention.

Something about nouns.

Do you approve of eggplant.

In *Practical Water,* in partial response to her own question as to what it is to live a moral life, Brenda Hillman writes, "An ethics occurs at the edge / of what we know // The creek goes underground about here." I am forced to consider my own example, greyer than my father's.

Roots aside, do you see yourself as having alignments, alliances, well-delineated antipathies, a sense of what you are in apposition with and opposition to as a writer.

Emily Dickinson said poetry was her letter to the world. Write me.

I read this poem in some magazine without writing down the poet's name. It pleased me, the second stanza esp.:

from DREADLOCKS

for *Jean-Michel Basquiat*

All the colors
wired together
so when he
combs his hair
the train explodes.

(Years later I uncovered the attribution: Elaine Equi.)

Does weather matter to poetry. Is it always night. Can we count on a sluggish ooze of light. Dream's mildew.

Linda Norton wrote that she "walked into poetry / in search of a place to rest, / a place to suffer formally"; Jack Gilbert remarked that poetry helps you to suffer more efficiently. Some comfort can be found in that.

Does poetry protect anything from anyone or any one from any thing.

Water seeks to get in as does poetry. True or false.

Compose a self-portrait in fewer than 12 lines. Fewer than 9. Fewer than 3.

Simone Weil wrote that a mind enclosed in language is in prison.

Handwritten annotations:

ooze of light. Dream is m
— C.D. Wright
oh fuck, oh fuck
I dreamt
all was ooze, all
was mildew, black sp
for everyone and
light?
Light, in chains,
when spread under a board, except
facelen uniforms
asking

from where did v
come?
who sent
here?

Apply a crèche, an exaltation, a float, a skein, or smack of adjectives to your poetry.

Returning to this matter of form, Czeslaw Milosz said that form in poetry has many uses; one of them is, like refrigeration, to preserve bad meat. Think of better uses. Be specific.

"If not a writer, then I would probably be a geologist. I majored in geology, was heading to graduate school in paleontology, and then the doe-eyed dark angel touched my shoulder with a finger and the doctor said, third-stage melanoma, let's go. In no time, I'd lost my spleen, a line of lymph nodes, a bear's mouthful of flesh and muscle over my shoulder blade, and a rectangle of skin, about the size of a City Lights paperback, that had been stripped for use as a graft. Lying in the hospital, nothing but words in my head, I began to imagine another way to love the earth, and to find something to stand on," wrote Forrest Gander in response to the question, If not a writer…

Even if it is nothing except fishes, on what will you stand.

So my singing nemesis, where do we go from here.

Thinking of an Arthur Sze poem that opens,

> "Fuck you, *fuck you*," he repeated as he drove down the dirt road
> while tamarisk branches scraped the side of the pickup;

I wonder why I take such pleasure in that invective. In this case it partly has to do with what soon follows, including the synesthetic,

> who hears the night-blooming cereus
> unfold a white blossom by the windowsill?

I like a high contrast, and he is particularly prone to pulling that off, though this is just one of scores of his examples.

Do you want to tell me a secret.

When you feel that gravitational pull, release your fleet of dreams.

Do you prefer warmer or cooler, blended or bent tones.

Matthew Arnold said that at bottom poetry is a criticism of life. Do you agree this is a function of the art. What then. Give reasons.

Anthocyanins make a beech leaf purple and strawberries red. Though vertebrates do not contain the pigment, what makes you so blue. Granted, color is subjective.

Grandma Wright completed fourth grade; the school year was
under 100 days; I don't know how far she walked to attend; I
know her trousseau was composed of rough, simple cloth, including
laundered, folded, and bleached flour sacks; I know she raised five sons and acres
and acres of tomatoes;
her husband Robert and a son drove the tomatoes to Eureka Springs in a wagon
and sold them for $8 a ton; the favorite son, the bright, blue-eyed, wavy-haired blond
Audie, was shot down over Southern Italy in 1943;
he and my brilliant,
honorable father Ernie Edward had planned to open a law office together after
the war,
and no family member ever fully recovered from Audie's death. If the one-room house
still stands, the hillside is overtaken by thorn trees, and the peonies Grandmother Wright
planted as a young bride. This was the only record LuVindie Wright, née a Williams,
chronicled in her Self-Pronouncing New Testament; it is
my favorite found poem:

End Sheet

Harley Wright oprated on Ap 23, 1966

Ernie Wright and Aline Collins was married Friday Aug 22, 1941

Noah that built the ark was 950 years old when he died

Hot water heater was put in Jan 18, 1954

Even if it is nothing except fishes, on w[o]
will you stand — C.D. Wright
This standing

                    I stand, do you
stand, do we
stand

            on acorns?
little ship
            with a hat
what safe harbour
from squirrels . . . .

        little spinning top
what flat-top
~~table~~
            could hold you
~~you~~ weight —
what you dream
                    to be . . . . .

        little seed, little dreamer
I want to bury
you. I want
the earth
            to take you
break you. big & bigger

you, I want to want
+ stay so legit in my
standing you will grow
blend pwr
little, poso, meist + carry me for years.
litter.

Among the Poetry Books Quoted

Cha, Theresa Hak Kyung. *Dictée*. Tanam Press, 1982; Third Woman Press, 1995; University of California Press, 2001.

Char, René. *No Siege Is Absolute: Versions*. Translated by Franz Wright. Lost Roads Publishers, 1984.

Connell, Evan S. *Points for a Compass Rose*. Alfred A. Knopf, 1973; North Point Press, 1985; Counterpoint, 2012.

Creeley, Robert. *The Collected Poems of Robert Creeley, 1975–2005*. University of California Press, 2006.

Equi, Elaine. *Decoy*. Coffee House Press, 1994.

Gander, Forrest. *Eye Against Eye*. New Directions, 2005.

H.D. *Heliodora* (1924) and *Trilogy* (1946) in *Collected Poems, 1912–1944*. New Directions, 1986.

Hillman, Brenda. *Practical Water*. Wesleyan University Press, 2009.

———. *Seasonal Works with Letters On Fire*. Wesleyan University Press, 2013.

Lentine, Genine. *Mr. Worthington's Beautiful Experiments on Splashes*. New Michigan Press, 2010.

Miller, Jane. *Midnights*. Saturnalia Books, 2007.

Ondaatje, Michael. *Handwriting*. Alfred A. Knopf, 1999.

Oppen, George. *New Collected Poems*. New Directions, 2002.

Sze, Arthur. *Quipu*. Copper Canyon Press, 2005.

Taggart, John. *Is Music: Selected Poems*. Copper Canyon Press, 2010.

Valentine, Jean. *Door in the Mountain: New and Collected Poems, 1965–2003*. Wesleyan University Press, 2004.

Weinberger, Eliot. *9/12: New York After*. Prickly Paradigm Press, 2003.

Williams, William Carlos. *Spring and All*. Contact Editions, 1923; New Directions, 2011.

Wright, C.D. *One Big Self: An Investigation*. Copper Canyon Press, 2007.

Xi Chuan. *Notes on the Mosquito: Selected Poems*. Translated by Lucas Klein. New Directions, 2012.

Zurita, Raúl. *Purgatory*. (*Purgatorio,* 1979.) Translated by Anna Deeny. University of California Press, 2009.

About the Author

C.D. Wright is the author of more than a dozen books, most recently, *One With Others [a little book of her days]*, which won the National Book Critics Circle Award and the Lenore Marshall Poetry Prize and was a finalist for the National Book Award. Intended as a tribute to a radically iconoclastic friend, it also revolves around a particular series of events in the Arkansas Delta in 1969. A limited edition of her long poem *Breathtaken*, with linocuts by Walter Feldman, was published by Brown/Ziggurat Press in 2012. Her book *Rising, Falling, Hovering* won the 2009 International Griffin Poetry Prize. This work was situated along fault lines within the family, the beginning of the second Iraq war, illegal border crossings, the response on Mexico's streets to the U.S. bombings of Baghdad, and Mexico's magnetism despite enormous external and internal pressures. With photographer Deborah Luster she published *One Big Self: Prisoners of Louisiana*, which won the Lange-Taylor Prize from the Center for Documentary Studies at Duke University. On a fellowship for writers from the Wallace Foundation Wright curated a "walk-in book of Arkansas," a multimedia exhibition that toured throughout her native state. In 2004 she was named a MacArthur Fellow, and in 2005 she received the Robert Creeley Award. Wright is married to writer/translator Forrest Gander. They have a son, Brecht. She teaches at Brown University and lives outside of Providence.

 Poetry is vital to language and living. Since 1972, Copper Canyon Press has published extraordinary poetry from around the world to engage the imaginations and intellects of readers, writers, booksellers, librarians, teachers, students, and donors.

WE ARE GRATEFUL FOR THE MAJOR SUPPORT PROVIDED BY:

THE PAUL G. ALLEN
FAMILY FOUNDATION

Anonymous

John Branch

Diana Broze

Beroz Ferrell & The Point, LLC

Janet and Les Cox

Mimi Gardner Gates

Linda Gerrard and Walter Parsons

Gull Industries, Inc.
on behalf of William and Ruth True

Mark Hamilton and Suzie Rapp

Carolyn and Robert Hedin

Steven Myron Holl

Lakeside Industries, Inc.
on behalf of Jeanne Marie Lee

Maureen Lee and Mark Busto

TO LEARN MORE ABOUT UNDERWRITING
COPPER CANYON PRESS TITLES,
PLEASE CALL 360-385-4925 EXT. 103

WE ARE GRATEFUL FOR THE MAJOR SUPPORT PROVIDED BY:

OFFICE OF ARTS & CULTURE
SEATTLE

ART WORKS.

National
Endowment
for the Arts
arts.gov

WASHINGTON STATE
ARTS COMMISSION

Brice Marden

Ellie Mathews and Carl Youngmann as The North Press

H. Stewart Parker

Penny and Jerry Peabody

John Phillips and Anne O'Donnell

Joseph C. Roberts

Cynthia Lovelace Sears and Frank Buxton

The Seattle Foundation

Kim and Jeff Seely

David and Catherine Eaton Skinner

Dan Waggoner

C.D. Wright and Forrest Gander

Charles and Barbara Wright

The dedicated interns and faithful volunteers of Copper Canyon Press

The Chinese character for poetry is made up of two parts: "word"
and "temple." It also serves as pressmark for
Copper Canyon Press.

The poems are set in Fournier. Headings are set in Hightower Italic.
Printed on archival-quality paper.
Book design and composition by Phil Kovacevich.

← Violence in... poetry

p 90, 72

p.49 He was there to descern the declelen of huron thinking.

p.124 Queshmaid in January

p.4 This is the one scene where I advance determined, if not precisely ready, to do battle with what an overtly cited Jungian described as the anesthetized heart, the heart that does not react.

p.128 Linda Norton wrote that she "walked into poetry/ in search of a place to rest / a place to suffer formally; Jack Gilbert remarked that poetry helps you to suffer more efficiently.

POETRY
$18.00

The Poet, the Lion, Talking Pictures, El Farolito, a Wedding in St. Roch, the Big Box Store, the Warp in the Mirror, Spring, Midnights, Fire & All

C.D. Wright

Part study, part elliptical love song to poetics, MacArthur Fellow C.D. Wright's latest collection of prosimetrical essays argues that poetry is less a genre than a way of being and seeing. She rightfully insists that the answer to the many questions of poetry *is* poetry. Here, as in *Cooling Time,* a companion volume, Wright explores the province of poetic language in her own tricked-out literary ATV.

from "In a Word, a World"

I love them all.

I love that a handful, a mouthful, gets you by, a satchelful can land you a job, a well-chosen clutch of them could get you laid, and that a solitary word can initiate a stampede, and therefore can be formally outlawed — even by a liberal court bent on defending a constitution guaranteeing unimpeded utterance…. More than the pristine, I love the filthy ones for their descriptive talent as well as transgressive nature. I love the dirty ones more than the minced, in that I respect extravagant expression more than reserved. I admire reserve, especially when taken to an ascetic nth…. My relationship to the word is anything but scientific; it is a matter of faith on my part, that the word endows material substance, by setting the thing named apart from all else. *Horse*, then, unhorses what is not horse.

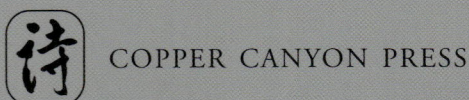

COPPER CANYON PRESS

ISBN 978-1-55659-485-4

Cover art: Denny Moers, *Black Bush in Desert, #1*
Author photo: Forrest Gander
Book design: Phil Kovacevich